Confucius said of the *I Ching*:

> "Is not the *I* a perfect book? . . . The *I* opens up the knowledge of the issues of things, accomplishes the undertakings of men, and embraces under it the way of all things under the sky. . . .
>
> "The sages made their emblematic symbols to set forth fully their ideas; appointed all the diagrams to show fully the truth and falsehood of things; appended their explanations to give the full expression of their words."

It is said that Confucius three times wore out the leather thongs that bound his copy of the *I Ching*, so often did he refer to it.

"Here hid, retired, cries out the crane;
Her young's responsive cry sounds there.
Of spirits good I drain this cup;
With thee a cup I'll freely share."

—James Legge,
I Ching

I CHING

The Chinese
BOOK OF CHANGES

arranged from the work of James Legge

by CLAE WALTHAM

AN ACE BOOK

Ace Publishing Corporation
1120 Avenue of the Americas
New York, N.Y. 10036

Printed in U.S.A.

CONTENTS

THIS ADAPTATION was suggested by a reference by James Legge to the way student editions of the *I Ching* appeared in China: with the ten wings drawn into the main body of the text.

GRATEFUL ACKNOWLEDGMENT is made to the Clarendon Press for permission to make use of the material in this way, to change the original romanization, and to abridge the complete work.

THIS VERSION has presented tasks of complexity and detail. Every effort has been made to keep errors of transliteration to a minimum, and to simplify avoidable complications. For what inaccuracies remain, due apology is made.

CHINA'S *Book of Changes,*
A SPHERICAL VIEW

I Ching, China's *Book of Changes*

A SPHERICAL VIEW

Probably no literary work has been spoken of in as many contradictory ways as this sacred book of ancient China.

It has been called the oldest extant writing in the world, China's unique heritage, and a great treasure for all mankind. It has also been dismissed as necromancy, a fortune-telling book, a mere manual for the practice of calligraphy.

In some centuries scholars have advised readers to delay their study of it until old age. In others, editors have prepared juvenile editions.

It has been described as both nonsense and wisdom, and many things in between. It is sometimes thought of as an oracle book, and sometimes as a book of religion. It contains a story of creation which is a first statement, such as our story of creation in Genesis. With remarkable brevity it binds into one skein man's origins, first inventions, and aspirations. It has served as history, guide, prophecy—a synthesis of past, present, and future.

Twenty-five centuries ago Confucius said, "If some

years were added to my life, I would give fifty to the study of the *I*,"—as he always called this book, with both familiarity and affection—"and might then escape falling into great errors."

Writing in 1937, Lady Dorothea Hosie relates that Confucius three times wore out the leather thongs that bound his copy. She described the *I* as a "curious and difficult collection of astrological and semi-transcendental maxims, which still attracts and puzzles the students of Chinese literature."

In the western hemisphere, the *I* has usually been entirely ignored, or dismissed as quaintly superstitious. The few who sought to penetrate its meaning were frequently defeated. It has taken us a long time to begin the approach to a sympathetic understanding of Chinese culture. One of the problems has been the existence of several different systems of romanization from the Chinese characters into English. Further contributing to the myth of the "Chinese puzzle" has been the fact that their great men are mentioned by several different names. The man we commonly know as Confucius may also be referred to as Ch'iu; K'ung; K'ung Ch'iu; Chung-ni; K'ung-Fe-Tse—and more than likely, a few others! When we consider that each can be romanized according to a different system of romanization, we can see that the language barrier has been as formidable as the Chinese wall.

But today we live in an era of atomic enlightenment. A rising generation is dedicated to the ways of peace through mutual understanding. A newer method of transliteration, the Yale romanization, is a simplification which incorporates a guide for pronunciation. In the new *Random House Dictionary of the English Language*, the *I Ching* is explicated in the main alphabet for a general public as "an ancient Chinese book of divination, in which 64 pairs of 8 symbols are shown with various interpretations. Also called *Book of Changes.*" Names and illustrations of the eight trigrams are also given, in the Wade-Giles method of transliteration but without diacritical marks over certain of the letters. In this modernization, such accent marks have also been dropped, as they are more apt to hinder than help the reader. A guide to general pronunciations is included in the alphabetical reference at the back.

The new generation is aware that China holds in her hand a pearl of great value, polished for more than fifty centuries until it reflects a consciousness that is cosmic. As the processes of change and transformation described in the *I* continue to work their secret operations this pearl now appears, now lies hidden, now reappears in the course of events taking place in the great business of life—to borrow some of the idiom used in the pages of the *I.*

When we compare Fu Hsi and the eight trigrams to Moses and the Ten Commandments we find ourselves right in the middle of the understanding gap between East and West. As we read in the *I,* Fu Hsi

". . . devised the eight trigrams to show fully the attributes of the spirit-like and intelligent operations working secretly, and to classify the qualities of the myriads of things."

These eight trigrams could be used to symbolize anything the human mind conceived of. The sixty-four hexagrams carry them through their logical combinations to the ultimate permutations. They represent "the denomination of that which cannot be denominated."

They are both immediate and practical, abstract and theoretical. In today's phrase we might call them open-ended. The school of thought they ultimately led to, Taoism, embodies the process of change as the core of its concept. Whoever first said that the more things change the more they are the same could have been describing the Chinese continuum that begins with Fu Hsi and is discernible today.

The Ten Commandments of Moses, however, represent a closed-end concept. The decalogue does not follow the "course of things" but seeks to establish its own course. It is not a continuum; it is not a process; it is a set of regulations so literally set down that no expansion and contraction is possible.

The two principles in the *I Ching*, the yang and the yin, represent the expansion and the contraction. These can also be designated heaven and earth, or Ch'ien and K'un. A sagely phrase for the genesis of this concept is the Great Extreme, from which came the Elementary Forms, which produced the Emblematic Symbols, which again produced the Eight Trigrams, from which were assembled the Sixty-Four Hexagrams. From its beginnings, Chinese thought has accepted a state of flux in all things. Change and transformation is the result of endless production and reproduction, reflected in nature, in man, in the inward mind.

Meaning, in Chinese, is not only subject to both expansion and contraction. Meaning can inhabit either the positive field or the negative. For instance, to speak of the time with "a sage upon the throne" indicates a condition of the highest good for the greatest number. But to speak of the throne *without* a sage upon it conveys a meaning just as concrete. Lao-Tzu, in speaking of a simple bowl such as might be used for mixing, observes that the use of the bowl depends on *what is not*. This mode of thought has been a further hindrance to mutual understanding between East and West, as we in the West tend to limit reality to what can be demonstrated in concrete terms.

The Chinese mind was from its beginnings used to thinking in concepts. This can be likened to four dimensional thinking as opposed to linear thinking. One kind moves back upon itself; the other travels outward in planes. We have been very much influenced in our culture by Euclid and the planes. The Chinese have been very much influenced in their culture by natural phenomena and the solids.

Perhaps related to the *I Ching Book of Changes*, certainly recognized as an ancient heritage, is T'ai Chi Chuan, literally translated as "perfect boxing." It is a form of total calisthenics gaining adherents all over the world. It controls the mind and induces harmony with the body through a series of continuous motions and gestures worked out in complete silence—a kind of yoga, or ballet without music. There are some people who believe that this T'ai Chi developed along with the *I Ching Book of Changes* as a visual explanation and participation in pantomime.

When we were still considering the earth flat, and feared to set out upon the ocean because we thought we might sail over the edge, the Chinese had long been thinking of the earth as a cube. Perhaps they never conceived of it in any way except four dimensional. *Four* dimensional because, in addition to the usual directions of north, east, south and west, the Chinese named a fifth: the center.

This has given the Chinese a spherical mode of thinking. Within spherical thinking man does not fear extremes because he can feel confident that no matter how far he travels he will probably meet himself coming back. Infinity, then, is a line that passes through him—as opposed to a vague theoretical line in the sky defined as having no beginning and no end.

Perhaps as a consequence of this, the Chinese have been able to make practical use of "extremes" while we have always distrusted them. Without extremes, they would have been much longer in explicating their doctrine of the *mean,* which is moderation, and of the *due* mean which is the *moderate* application of the practice of moderation, without which moderation can become a corruption. This brings us to the *enantiodromia* concept of C. G. Jung's: ". . . sooner or later everything runs into its opposite . . ."

Throughout the *I* such concepts are approximated, hinted at, intimated, pictured, symboled, and articulated in such constantly recurring terms as "firm and correct," "the superior man," "cross the great stream," and others. These phrases embody education, conduct, control of motivation, "divining" in the sense of psychological cybernetics. A form of early image-psychology is reflected in Hexagram 12 when the *I* warns its users to beware saying "I die! I die!" lest their fortunes be tied to a bushy clump.

The concepts and symbols of the *I,* strung along the phrases used again and again, rang in the ears of children as they ran out to play Mongols and Mandarins and were still ringing there when they came to ponder them in silence and reverence during their old age. Through these phrases the sagely person learns the basic integrity called "firm correctness," and knows that the "superior man" *is* firm correctness—but that firm correctness should not be carried to the utmost (Hexagram 18). Nothing catches the emergence of *tao* as clearly as the concept of changes. Within spherical thought all concepts are part of one sustaining rhizome.

We who cannot read Chaucer without special study, and who stand almost entirely severed from the Anglo Saxon Chronicle, endure a certain rootlessness. There is a gap between us and our beginnings that the Western Bible only imperfectly bridges.

A modern Chinese today reads in the *I* the wisdom that "If important matters in the germ be not kept secret, that will be injurious to their accomplishment," (Confucius, interpreting Line 1 of Hexagram 60). And this modern Chinese reads this in the very same characters read by Confucius. He can also look at an urn cast in bronze centuries before Christ and recognize characters still used in his own day. Such a man inherits a body of learning, a union of harmonies, along with his genes.

The wisdom of the *Book of Changes* constantly revolves before its readers, revealing the transformations of Tao which swirl about us whether we are aware or not. To one who is aware—to one who seeks, knocks, and asks, the gate swings open; its secret operations pour out in generous proportion.

But to one who does not seek, nor knocks, nor asks, the wisdom of *I* lies hid, a dragon in the deep, and there is no time of active doing. "Active doing" requires an expanded consciousness; a participation in truth. The *I* is representative of one great eternal truth which we can claim in our own names because in our own names that great truth long ago claimed us. Infinity stretches out, yes. But infinity also reaches in, yes. As the sages of old China saw the world as a vast cube rather than a vast plane, so their thought expanded to inhabit the many dimensions which embrace psychic thought as well as material objects, and came to know all things for what they are and not as something else—where all that is, was. In the fleeting moment of the Eternal Now, the Great Extreme reaches out to embrace the cosmos and then comes home again to lie like a pearl in an open palm.

Reflected in this pearl is the spherical view that James Legge caught in his magical vision.

James Legge was born in Scotland in 1815. For three years he was associated with the Anglo-Chinese College at Malacca, and for thirty years after it relocated at Hong Kong. In 1876 Oxford University constituted a chair of Chinese literature and language for his occupation. He died at Oxford in 1897.

Over a span of twenty-five years (1861-86), Legge published his translations of the *Chinese Classics*, for which he was awarded the Julien Prize of the French Institute. This was a complete transliteration into English of the sacred books of China, a voluminous work. His introductions to the various volumes convey the impression of a scholar who refuses to be hurried, but is nevertheless carried forward by the inner momentum of the task undertaken.

In 1854 he had begun work on the classic of *Changes*, which he called *Yi King*, and which was later to be more popularly known as *I Ching*. No translation of this book existed in English at the time he wrote. Some of his romanizations are no longer in popular usage. In this version they have been changed to the Wade-Giles system. Also, the Yale system of romanization is given within parentheses in the alphabetical reference. Legge was breaking new ground. His divisions of the diagrams into trigrams and hexagrams set a precedent all later translators have followed. One feels strongly that a scholar of his ilk would be the first to advocate changes in a work of changes—one that had in every century hordes of editors and authors and yet, by its own secret operations of change and transformation, remained the same. His spelling has been both Americanized and brought up to date, and his scrupulous presentation of debatable points has been abridged.

Legge not only had all of the usual handicaps of a pioneer, but he had the misfortune of having the completed manuscript of the *I Ching* soaked for more than a month in the Red Sea. He states:

"By dint of careful manipulation it was recovered so as to be still legible; but it was not till 1874 that I began to be able to give to the book the prolonged attention necessary to make it reveal its secrets. Then for the first time I got hold, as I believe, of the clue, and found that my toil of twenty years before was of no service at all. . . . How to surmount this difficulty occurred to me after I had found the clue to the interpretation . . . namely, that the written characters of the Chinese are not representations of words, but symbols of ideas, and that the combination of them in composition is not a representation of what the writer would say, but of what he thinks. . . . In the study of a Chinese classical book there is not so much an interpretation of the characters employed by the writer as a participation of his thoughts;—there is the seeing of mind to mind. . . ."

More vicissitudes were in store. He was attacked by his contemporaries because he translated the Chinese concepts of Ti and Shang Ti as God. His colleagues in the missionary field objected to this and, in 1880, to quote Legge again:

" . . . twenty-three gentlemen addressed a letter to Professor F. Max Müller, complaining that, in . . . a work edited by him, he should allow me to give my own private interpretation of the name or names in question . . . but when I examined the question . . . with all possible interest and all the resources at my command, I came to the conclusion that Ti, on its first employment by the Chinese fathers, was intended to express the same concept which our fathers expressed by God. . . . I am translating, and not giving a private interpretation of my own . . ."

The climate of the day was provincial, bigoted, and rigid. Legge was, moreover, active in the missionary field. Nevertheless, he refused to yield. Today it might be called a decision; in 1880 it was an act of courage. In Volume XVI of the *The Sacred Books of the East*, under the general editorship of F. Max Müller, Ti and Shang Ti were again translated as God.

There are those who maintain even today that there is no "God" in the proper sense of Chinese religion. But what about that which "is the denomination of what cannot be denominated"? Perhaps this is a reverence so expressive that we have missed its meaning. And while we think of Zen as Japanese, it was in China as Ch'an that it ripened. Chinese religious thought is like a ship: long after it has passed, its waves still beat upon the shore.

Legge remained the enlightened Sinologue and

aroused scholar. Throughout his work his copious annotations set forth his reasoning. His translation of the *I Ching* stands as a monument of objectivity, his scholarship so coolly explicated that readers are forced to reach their own, subjective conclusions. His translation is the platform that has girded later translations and many interpretations. His natural ambience was ahead of his time, and gave him unusual insight into Chinese spherical thinking. His doctrinal upbringing constantly warred with what his subtle vision kept catching. Strewn along his compendious footnotes are many evidences of desperate, seesawing battles that took place between his head and his heart, his thinking and his intuition, his rationality and his feeling. But always, in the end, his harmonies exceeded his conflicts. His natural ambience allowed him to be both objective and respectful, an unusual combination among pioneers, and it is this quality in his work that keeps his translation relevant and illuminating today.

Legge places the legendary reign of Fu Hsi in the thirty-fourth century B.C. He places the *I Ching* within traceable history during the twelfth century B.C., and adduces its origin to an earlier time. With the possible exceptions of the books of the Pentateuch, Joshua, and Judges, he feels that an equal antiquity cannot be claimed for any portion of the sacred scriptures of the West.

Western scholars still puzzle over problems of interpolation within the Bible, but in the *I* accretions to the original text are contained within what are known as the ten wings, and these Legge arranged into seven appendices. New translations, and annotations amounting to scholarly debates and learned essays, are but further accretions. The *I* has had innumerable editors, and the corruptions inevitable in the preservation of an ancient document.

But something in the *I* cannot be tampered with; something in the *I* speaks across the centuries from an incorruptible core.

The *I* stands on its own feet. Jules Mohl, fellow Orientalist, said of it to Legge, "I like it; for I come to it out of a sea of mist, and find solid ground." But most of us are not familiar with the Chinese language, and few of us are scholars. We are apt to come to the *I* from solid ground and find there a sea of mist. Often we find the accretions from its many editors, and the enrichment of scholarly footnotes, an encumbrance to our enjoyment and understanding. Unless one were a student, the manuscript might just as well have remained in the waters of the Red Sea.

But the major hindrance to the West's understanding of the *I*, perhaps, may be because the work is presented backward, without due thought to the fact that the Chinese read their books and scrolls from right to left instead of, as we do, from left to right. Upon first opening the *I*, the Western reader soon is brought face to face with the hexagrams, and their enigmatic explanations. The story of the *I*'s origin, explanations of the trigrams, and other explanatory material, appear later. We are on page 382 of Legge before we encounter the illuminating passage which begins "Anciently, when Fu Hsi had come to the rule of all under heaven . . ." and read of the origin of the diagrams.

Probably Confucius' first exploration of the *I* began at what we would call the back of the book. We cannot know for sure at what point he took up his study of it. But we do know he too found solid ground there. He is quoted as saying:

". . . Is not the *I* a perfect book? . . . The *I* opens up the knowledge of the issues of things, accomplishes the undertakings of men, and embraces under it the way of all things under the sky . . . Thereby the sages, through divination by it, would give their proper course to the aims of all under the sky, would give stability to their undertakings, and determine their doubts. . . . Is it impossible then to discover the ideas of the sages? . . . The sages made their emblematic symbols to set forth fully their ideas; appointed all the diagrams to show fully the truth and falsehood of things; appended their explanations to give the full expression of their words . . . They thus stimulated the people as by drums and dances . . ."

The aim of this version of the *I Ching* is to uncover the solid ground of the *I Ching*. For this purpose it has been modernized, rearranged, and abridged.

Legge feels that many incongruous ideas worked their way into the *I* during the six hundred or seven hundred years which separated the twelfth century Text from the appendices. Selections from these later accretions are given after the Text, as "From the Wings," and in the separate sections "Wen Yen Ch'uan" and "The Master Said."

I Ching as a book of divination is discussed on pages 85-102.

Basic to understanding the *I* is understanding the concept of yang and yin.

YANG	YIN
bright	dark
sun-like	moon-like

YANG	YIN
the Great Brightness	the Great Obscurity
strong	weak
male	female
heaven	earth
hard	soft

The list of contraries is inexhaustible, and should also include positive and negative, conscious and unconscious. Yang is always represented as an undivided line: —. Yin is always represented by a divided line: - -. Legge most often, for his purposes, translates these symbolic lines as either strong or weak, undivided or divided. For the purposes of this modern version, undivided lines are often referred to as yang, and the divided lines are referred to as yin—as an aid in keeping the basic concept in mind.

Yang is not superior to yin, nor is yin superior to yang. Legge mentions the equivalence of the symbolic names:

"The connection of the two is necessary to the production of one substantial thing. The yang originates a shadowy outline which the yin fills up with a definite substance."

The reader is further referred to Illustration A. If the long history of the *I* tells us anything, it is that it unfolds its meaning through individual insight and not by rote. One who studies the *I* discovers his own I, and not the I of another.

Because of this the *I* is a book to read, to meditate upon, and to discover one's identity in. A book, in the words of Confucius, "not to be let slip from the mind."

"ILLUSTRATION A"

"The connection of the two is necessary to the
production of one substantial thing."

By study of the *I* one develops a sagely personhood. Incidental to this he learns to "make speed without haste," and discovers the secret springs of things through such wisdom as the essay on righteousness:

The great attribute of heaven and earth is the giving and maintaining life. What is most precious for the sage is to get the highest place in which he can be the human representative of heaven and earth. What will guard his position for him? Men. How shall he collect a large population round him? By the power of his wealth.

The right administration of that wealth, correct instructions to the people, and prohibitions against wrong-doings, these constitute his righteousness.

Here is the theme of the *I Ching* in a sequence that leads from Fu Hsi through the 64th hexagram. Those who do not wish to become students of the *I Ching* will have an idea of its content, and a wider view of the Chinese people. For those who will become students of the *I*, this is offered not as a substitute to complete work, but as an avenue leading toward it.

It is the remarkable achievement of James Legge that he opened a window to China, the real China, the China that has endured and will continue to endure. It is a very small window that is open now, that is true. Still, it is a window, and it is open, and there is no limit on what can come through that window because it is a window of the mind.

And it begins here, now, in this vestige of the ancient past you hold in your hands: Changes.

—Clae Waltham

```
      C
      H
      A
CHANGES
      G
      E
      S
```

from James Legge's translation of the *I Ching*, Part II of "The Texts of Confucianism"; from Volume XVI of "The Sacred Books of the East" edited by F. Max Müller.

ANCIENTLY THE SAGES

ANCIENTLY THE SAGES

Five great men of antiquity lead the way in the various steps of the progress, guided by the I; 3400-2200 B.C. The writer gives the legends current in his own time about the various inventions, and connects them with certain hexagrams.

I is the character that symbolizes change. It is formed from the character for "the sun" placed over that for "the moon." As the sun gives place to the moon, and the moon to the sun, so is change always proceeding in the phenomena of nature and the experiences of society.

The I is fashioned to give us a picture of the phenomena of the external universe. The writer supposes a constant change from rest to movement and from movement to rest, through which all things are formed, now still, now in motion, now expanding, now contracting: "the course of things."

—James Legge,
I Ching.

Anciently, when Fu Hsi had come to the rule of all under heaven, looking up, he contemplated the brilliant forms exhibited in the sky, and looking down he surveyed the patterns shown on the earth. He contemplated the ornamental appearances of birds and beasts and the different suitabilities of the soil. Near at hand, in his own person, he found things for consideration, and the same at a distance, in things in general. On this he devised the eight trigrams to show fully the attributes of the spirit-like and intelligent operations working secretly, and to classify the qualities of the myriads of things.

He invented the making of nets of various kinds by knitting strings, both for hunting and fishing. The idea of this suggests Li, the third trigram and thirtieth hexagram.

On the death of Fu Hsi, there arose Shen Nung. He fashioned wood to form the share, and bent wood to make the plow handle. The advantages of plowing and weeding were then taught to all under heaven. The idea of this suggests I, the forty-second hexagram.

He caused markets to be held at midday, thus bringing together all the people, and assembling in one place all their wares. They made their exchanges and retired, every one having got what he wanted. The idea of this suggests Shih Ho, the twenty-first hexagram.

After the death of Shen Nung, there arose Huang Ti, Yao, and Shun. They carried through the changes, so that the people did what was required of them without being wearied; yea, they exerted such a spirit-like transformation that the people approved their ordinances. When a series of changes has run all its courses, another change ensues.

When a series of changes obtains free course, it will continue long. Hence it was that "these sovereigns were helped by Heaven; they had good fortune, and their every movement was advantageous."

Huang Ti, Yao and Shun wore their upper and lower garments simply, as patterns to the people, and good order was secured for all under heaven. The idea of this suggests the trigrams Ch'ien and K'un, Heaven and Earth, and the first and second hexagrams.

They hollowed out trees to form canoes; they cut others long and thin to make oars. Thus arose the benefit of canoes and oars for the help of those who had no means of intercourse with others. They could now reach the most distant parts, and all under heaven were benefited. The idea of this suggests Huan, the fifty-ninth hexagram.

They used oxen in carts and yoked horses to chariots, thus providing for the carriage of what was heavy, and for distant journeys, thereby benefiting all under the sky. The idea of this suggests Sui, the seventeenth hexagram.

They built the defense of double gates, and the warning sound of the clapper, as a preparation against the approach of marauders. The idea of this suggests Yu, the sixteenth hexagram.

They cut wood and fashioned it into pestles; they dug in the ground and formed mortars. Thus myriads of the people received the benefit arising from the use of the pestle and mortar. The idea of this suggests Hsiao Kuo, the sixty-second hexagram.

They bent wood by means of string to form bows, and sharpened wood to make arrows. This served to produce everywhere a feeling of awe. The idea of this suggests K'uei, the thirty-eighth hexagram.

In the highest antiquity they made their homes in winter caves, and in summer dwelt in the open country. In subsequent ages, the sages substituted houses with the ridge-beam above and the projecting roof below, as a provision against wind and rain. The idea of this suggests Ta Chuang, the thirty-fourth hexagram.

When the ancients buried their dead, they covered the body thickly with pieces of wood, having laid it in the open country. They raised no mound over it, nor planted trees around. Nor had they any fixed period of mourning. In subsequent ages the sages substituted for these practices the inner and outer coffins. The idea of this suggests Ta Kuo, the twenty-eighth hexagram.

In the highest antiquity, government was carried on successfully by the use of knotted cords to preserve the memory of things. In subsequent ages the sages substituted for these written characters and bonds. By means of these the doings of all the officers could be regulated, and the affairs of all the people accurately examined. The idea of this suggests Kuai, the forty-third hexagram.

The I was made on a principle of accordance with heaven and earth, and shows us therefore, without rent or confusion, the course of things in heaven and earth. The sage in accordance with the I knows the causes of darkness and that which is obscure. He knows the causes of light and that which is bright. He traces things to their beginning, and follows them to their end; thus he knows what can be said about death and life. He perceives the union of essence and breath, and the wandering away of the soul.

There is a similarity between the sage and heaven and earth, and no contrariety in him to them. His knowledge embraces all things, and his course is intended to be helpful to all under the sky; hence he falls into no error. He acts according to the exigency of circumstances without being carried away by their current; he rejoices in heaven and knows its ordinations; and hence he has no anxieties. He rests in his own place, and cherishes the spirit of generous benevolence; hence he can love without reserve.

Through the I, the sage comprehends as in a mold or enclosures the transformations of heaven and earth. He penetrates to a knowledge of the course of day and night, and all connected phenomena. It is thus that his operation is spirit-like, unconditioned by place, while the changes which he produces are not restricted to any form.

The successive movement of the inactive and active operations constitutes what is called the course of things.

That which ensues as the result of their movement is goodness; that which shows it in its completeness is the nature of men and things.

The benevolent see it and call it benevolence. The wise see it and call it wisdom. The common people, acting daily according to it, yet have no knowledge of it. Thus it is that the course of things, as seen by the superior man, is seen by few.

It is manifested in the benevolence of its operations,

and then again it conceals and stores up its resources. It gives their stimulus to all things, without having the same anxieties that possess the sage. Complete is its abundant virtue and the greatness of its stores!

Its rich possession is what is intended by "the greatness of its stores"; the daily renovation which it produces is what is meant by "the abundance of its virtue."

Production and reproduction is what is called the process of change.

That which is unfathomable in the movement of the inactive and active operations is the presence of a spiritual power.

In the I there are four things characteristic of the way of the sages. We should set the highest value on its explanations to guide us in speaking; on its changes for the initiation of our movements; on its emblematic figures for definite action as in the construction of implements; and on its prognostications for our practice of divination.

Therefore, when a superior man is about to take action of a more private or of a public character, he asks the I, making his inquiry in words. It receives his order, and the answer comes as the echo's response. Be the subject remote or near, mysterious or deep, he forthwith knows of what kind will be the coming result. If the I were not the most exquisite thing under heaven, would it be concerned in such an operation as this?

In all these operations forming the I, there is no thought and no action. It is still and without movement; but, when acted on, it penetrates forthwith to all phenomena and events under the sky. If it were not the most spirit-like thing under the sky, how could it be found doing this?

The operations forming the I are the method by which

the sages searched out exhaustively what was deep, and investigated the minutest springs of things.

"Those operations searched out what was deep": therefore they could penetrate to the views of all under the sky. "They made apparent the minutest springs of things": therefore they could bring to a completion all undertakings under the sky. "Their action was spirit-like": therefore they could make speed without hurry, and reached their destination without traveling.

This is the import of what the Master said, that "In the I there are four things indicating the way of the sages."

In the system of the I, the two elementary forms are: — and - -. These are the yang and the yin.

They give birth to the four emblematic symbols, each one of two lines:

By the addition to each of these symbols first of the yang line (−), and then of the yin (- -), there arose the eight trigrams:

The sages made their emblematic symbols to set forth fully their ideas; appointed all the diagrams to show fully the truth and falsehood of things; appended their explanations to give the full expression of their words; and changed the various lines to exhibit fully what was advantageous. They thus stimulated the people as by drums and dances, thereby developing the spirit-like character of the I.

May we not say that the yang and the yin are the secret and substance of the I? It was yang and yin being established in their several places that the system of changes was thereby constituted.

The eight trigrams served to determine the good and evil issues of events, and from this determination was produced the successful prosecution of the great business of life.

The formation of the eight trigrams constitutes the small completion of the I.

THE TRIGRAMS

THE TRIGRAMS

The eight trigrams served to determine the good and evil issues of events, and from this determination was produced the successful prosecution of the great business of life.

—James Legge,
I Ching.

In the trigram, the first line represents earth; the second, man; and the third, heaven. These are the three Powers. (J.L.)

The Trigrams

Anciently, when the sages made the I, it was with the design that its figures should be in conformity with the principles underlying the natures of men and things, and the ordinances for them appointed by Heaven. With this view they exhibited in them the way of heaven, and of earth, calling the lines yin and yang; and the way of men under the names of benevolence and righteousness. Each trigram embraced those three Powers.

The symbols of heaven and earth·received their determinate positions; those for mountains and collections of water interchanged their influences; those for thunder and wind excited each other the more; and those for water and fire did each other no harm. Then among these eight symbols there was a mutual communication.

The eight trigrams communicate their information by their emblematic figures. The explanations appended to the lines and the completed figures tell how the contemplation of them affected the makers. The yang and the yin lines appear mixed in them, and thus the good and the evil which they indicate can be seen.

When we speak of Spirit we mean the subtle presence and operation of God with all things. For putting things in motion there is nothing more vehement than Thunder (Chen). For scattering them there is nothing more effective than Wind (Sun). For drying them up there is nothing more parching than Fire (Li). For giving them pleasure and satisfaction there is nothing more grateful than a lake or Marsh (Tui). For moistening them there is nothing more enriching than Water (K'an). For bringing them to an end and making them begin again there is nothing more fully adapted than a hill or Mountain (Ken). Thus water and fire contribute together to the one object; thunder and wind do not act contrary to each other; mountains and collections of water interchange their influences. It is in this way that they are able to change and transform, and to give completion to all things.

The Master said: "The trigrams Ch'ien and K'un may be regarded as the gate of the I. Ch'ien represents what is of the yang nature: bright and active; K'un what is of the yin nature: shaded and inactive. These two unite according to their qualities, and there comes the embodiment of the result by the yin and yang lines. In this way we have the phenomena of heaven and earth visibly exhibited, and can comprehend the operation of the spiritual intelligence."

Thus, a door shut may be pronounced analogous to K'un or the inactive condition, and the opening of the door analogous to Ch'ien or the active condition. The opening succeeding the being shut may be pronounced analogous to what we call a change; and the passing from one of these states to the other may be called the constant course of things.

Consider the trigram Ch'ien and the trigram K'un. If

Ch'ien and K'un were taken away there would be no means of seeing that system. Ch'ien and K'un would almost cease to act.

For the trigram of Ch'ien is the emblem of heaven, the trigram of K'un is the emblem of earth.

Ch'ien and K'un do nothing, and yet do everything; hence they are able to perfect the spirit-like subtlety of the action of thunder, wind, and other things.

TRIGRAMS IN THE ORDER ATTRIBUTED TO FU HSI:

CH'IEN, HEAVEN: the concentration of the yang force. Ch'ien is the symbol of heaven, and hence has the appellation of father.

Ch'ien suggests the idea of heaven; of a circle; of a ruler; of a father; of jade; of metal; of cold; of ice; of deep red; of a good horse; of an old horse; of a thin horse; of a piebald horse; and of the fruit of trees.

Ch'ien is creative force directing the great beginnings of things. Ch'ien is a door . . . open.

In Ch'ien, God struggles.

TUI, MARSH: The attributes of Tui are pleasure and satisfaction.

Tui suggests the emblem of a low-lying collection of water; of the youngest daughter; of a sorceress; of the mouth and tongue; of the decay and putting down of things in harvest; of the removal of fruits hanging from the stems or branches; among soils, of what is strong and salt; of a concubine; and of a sheep.

God rejoices in Tui.

LI, FIRE: The attributes of Li are brightness and intelligence. It also has the meaning of inhering in or adhering to: attachment. It is also called the trigram of elegance.

Li suggests the emblem of fire; of the sun; of lightning; of the second daughter; of buff-coat and helmet; of spear and sword. Referred to men, it suggests the large belly. It is the trigram of dryness. It suggests the emblem of a turtle; of a crab; of a spiral univalve; of the mussel; and of the tortoise. Referred to trees, it suggests one which is hollow and rotten above.

God's processes are manifested to one another in Li.

CHEN, THUNDER: The attribute of Chen is to put things in motion. To move and excite is the quality of Thunder. Chen is a motive force, denoting exciting power.

Chen suggests the idea of thunder; of the dragon; of the union of the azure and the yellow; of development; of a great highway; of the eldest son; of decision and vehemence; of bright young bamboos; of sedges and rushes; among horses, of the good neigher; of one whose white hind-leg appears, of the prancer, and of one with a white star in his forehead. Among the productions of husbandry it suggests the idea of what returns to life from its disappearance beneath the surface, of what in the end becomes the strongest, and of what is the most luxuriant.

God comes forth in Chen to do his producing work.

K'UN, EARTH: The concentration of the yin force. K'un is the symbol of earth, and hence has the appellation of mother.

K'un suggests the idea of the earth; of cloth; of a cauldron; of parsimony; of a turning lathe; of a young heifer; of a large wagon; of what is variegated; of a multitude; and of a handle and support. Among soils it denotes what is black.

K'un represents compendious receptivity, and responds to Ch'ien. K'un completes the great beginnings originated by Ch'ien. Think of a door . . . closed.

The greatest service to God is done for Him in K'un.

KEN, MOUNTAIN: The attributes of Ken are twofold; it is both active and passive, resting and arresting.

Ken suggests the emblem of a mountain, of a by-path; of a small rock; of a gateway; of the fruits of trees and creeping plants; of a porter or a eunuch; of the ring finger; of the dog; of the rat; of birds with powerful bills; among trees, of those which are strong, with many joints.

Ken suggests both the ending and the commencing of all things.

Ken is the symbol of mountain, the mass of which is still. It is regulatory in that it can "arrest"; stoppage.

God completes the work of the year in Ken.

K'AN, WATER: As a character it represents a "pit," a perilous cavity . . . a dangerous defile with water flowing through it.

K'an suggests the idea of water; of channels and ditches for draining and irrigation; of being hidden and lying concealed; of being now straight, and now crooked; of a bow, and of a wheel. As referred to man, it suggests the idea of an increase of anxiety; of distress of mind; of pain in the ears; it is the trigram of the blood; it suggests the idea of what is red. As referred to horses, it suggests the idea of the horse with an elegant spine; of one with a high spirit; of one with a drooping head;

of one with a thin hoof; and of one with a shambling step. As referred to carriages, it suggests one that encounters many risks. It suggests what goes right through; the moon; a thief. Referred to trees, it suggests that which is strong, and firm-hearted.

God is comforted and enters into rest in K'an.

SUN, WIND: The attributes of Sun are the "penetrating" and the "flexible."

Sun suggests the idea of wood; of wind; of the oldest daughter; of a plumb-line; of a carpenter's square; of being white; of being long; of being lofty; of advancing and receding; of want of decision; and of strong scents. It suggests in the human body, the idea of deficiency of hair; of a wide forehead; of a large development of the white of the eye. Among tendencies, it suggests the close pursuit of gain, even to making three hundred percent in the market. In the end it may become the trigram of decision.

Sun is the trigram of the advancing and the receding which denotes the processes of production, and the purity and equal arrangement of all things.

God brings His processes into full and equal action in Sun.

Among animals, Ch'ien suggests the idea of a horse; K'un that of an ox; Chen that of the dragon; Sun that of a fowl; K'an that of a pig; Li, that of a pheasant; Ken, that of a dog; and Tui, that of a sheep.

In the body, Ch'ien suggests the idea of the head; K'un, that of the belly; Chen, that of the feet; Sun, that of the thighs; K'an, that of the ears; Li, that of the eyes; Ken, that of the hands; and Tui, that of the mouth.

In the family, Ch'ien represents the father; K'un the mother.

Chen shows a first application of Ch'ien to K'un, resulting in getting the first of its male or yang lines, and hence is called "the oldest son." Sun shows a first application of Ch'ien to K'un, resulting in getting the first of its female or yin lines, and hence is called "the oldest daughter." K'an shows a second application of K'un to Ch'ien, resulting in getting the second of its male or yang lines, and hence is called "the second son." Li shows a second application of Ch'ien to K'un, resulting in getting the second of its female or yin lines, and hence is called "the second daughter." Ken shows a third application of K'un to Ch'ien, resulting in getting the third of its male or yang lines, and hence is called "the youngest son." Tui shows a third application of its female or yin lines, and hence is called "the youngest daughter."

Ch'ien is the symbol of strength; K'un of docility; Chen of stimulus to movement; Sun of penetration; K'an of what is precipitous and perilous; Li of what is bright and what is catching; Ken of stoppage or arrest; and Tui of pleasure and satisfaction.

Anciently, when the sages made the I, in order to give mysterious assistance to the spiritual Intelligences, they contemplated the changes in the divided and undivided lines and formed the trigrams; from the movements that took place in the yang and yin lines, they produced their teaching about the separate lines. There ensued a harmonious conformity to the course of duty and to virtue, with a discrimination of what was right in each particular case. They thus made an exhaustive discrimination of what was right, and effected the complete development of every nature, till they arrived in the I at what was appointed for it by Heaven.

Thunder serves to put things in motion; wind to scatter the genial seeds of them; rain to moisten them; the sun to warm them; what is symbolized by Ken, to arrest and keep them in their places; by Tui, to give them joyful course; by Ch'ien to rule them; and by K'un, to store them up.

The sun goes and the moon comes; the moon goes and the sun comes; the sun and moon thus take the place each of the other, and their shining is the result. The cold goes and the heat comes; the heat goes and the cold comes; it is by this mutual succession of the cold and heat that the year is completed. That which goes becomes less and less, and that which comes waxes more and more; it is by the influence on each other of this contraction and expansion that the advantages of the different conditions are produced.

God comes forth in Chen to His producing work; He brings His processes into full and equal action in Sun; they are manifested to one another in Li; the greatest service is done for Him in K'un; He rejoices in Tui; He struggles in Ch'ien; He is comforted and enters into rest in K'an; and He completes the work of the year in Ken.

WEN YEN CH'UAN

_____

Wen Yen Ch'uan

The Seventh Wing

To *wen* is given the meaning of "explaining," and to *yen* that of "words or sentences."

It was the assumption of Chu Hsi that the chronicler used the phraseology of "The Master said" to distinguish the real words of Confucius from more ancient sayings.

—James Legge,
I Ching.

Supplementary to the T'uan and the Yao on the first and second hexagrams, and showing how they may be interpreted of man's nature and doings. (J.L.)

CH'IEN

What is called under Ch'ien "the great and originating" is in man the first and chief quality of goodness. What is called "the penetrating" is the assemblage of excellences. What is called "the advantageous" is the harmony of all that is right. What is called "the correct and firm" is the faculty of action.

The superior man, embodying benevolence, is fit to preside over men. Presenting the assemblage of excellences, he is fit to show in himself the union of all propriety. Benefiting all creatures, he is fit to exhibit the harmony of all that is right. Correct and firm, he is fit to manage all affairs.

The fact that the superior man practices these virtues justifies the application to him of the words:

Ch'ien represents what is great and originating, penetrating, advantageous, correct and firm.

What is the meaning of the words under the first line, yang: "The dragon lies hid in the deep; it is not the time for active doing"?

The Master said: "There he is, with the powers of the dragon, and yet lying hid. The influence of the world would make no change in him. He would do nothing merely to secure his fame. He can live, withdrawn from the world, without regret. He can experience disapproval without trouble of mind. Rejoicing in opportunity, he carries his principles into action; sorrowing for want of opportunity, he keeps with them in retirement. Yes, he is not to be torn from his root in himself. This is 'the dragon lying hid.'"

What is the meaning of the words under the second line, "The dragon shows himself and is in the field; it will be advantageous to see the great man"?

The Master said: "There he is, with the dragon's powers, and occupying exactly the central place. He is sincere even in his ordinary words, and earnest in his ordinary conduct. Guarding against depravity, he preserves his sincerity. His goodness is recognized in the world, but he does not boast of it. His virtue is extensively displayed, and transformation ensues. The language of the I, 'The dragon shows himself and is in the field; it will be advantageous to see the great man' refers to a ruler's virtue."

What is the meaning of the words under the third line, "The superior man is active and vigilant all the day, and in the evening still careful and apprehensive; the position is dangerous, but there will be no mistake"?

The Master said: "The superior man advances in virtue, and cultivates all the sphere of his duty. Loyalty and good faith are the way by which he advances in virtue. His attention to his words, and establishing his sincerity are the way by which he occupies his sphere. He knows the utmost point to be reached and reaches it, thus showing himself in accord with the first springs of things. He knows the end to be rested in and rests in it, thus preserving his righteousness in accordance with that end. Therefore he occupies a high position without pride, and a low position without anxiety. Thus it is that being active and vigilant, and careful also and apprehensive as the time requires, though his position be perilous, he will make no mistake."

What is the meaning of the words under the fourth line, "He is as if he were leaping up, but still is in the deep; there will be no mistake"?

The Master said: "He finds no permanent place either above or below, but he does not commit the error of advancing. He may advance or recede; there is no permanent place for him; but he does not leave his fellows. The superior man, advancing in virtue and cultivating the sphere of his duty, yet wishes to advance only at the proper time, and therefore there is no mistake."

What is the meaning of the words under the fifth line, "The dragon is on the wing in the sky; it will be advantageous to see the great man"?

The Master said: "Notes of the same key respond to one another; creatures of the same nature seek one another; water flows toward the place that is low and damp; fire rises toward what is dry; clouds follow the dragon, and winds follow the tiger: so the sage makes his appearance, and all men look to him. Things that draw their origin from heaven move toward what is above; things that draw their origin from the earth cleave to what is below: so does everything follow its kind."

What is the meaning of the words under the topmost line, "The dragon exceeds the proper limits; there will be occasion for repentance"?

The Master said: "The position is noble, but it is not that of office; its occupant dwells on high, but he has no people to rule; and the men of talent and virtue in the positions below will give him no aid: should he move in such a case, there will be occasion for repentance."

Yang lines appear in all these representations of the great and originating power denoted by Ch'ien. What follows in the Yao tells us how all under the sky there will be good order. We see the model of action afforded by heaven.

The "greatness" and "originating" represented by Ch'ien refer to it as the symbol of what gives their beginning to all things, and also secures their growth and development.

"The advantageousness and the correctness and firmness" refer to its nature and feelings as seen in all the resulting things.

Ch'ien, thus originating, is able with its admirable benefits to benefit all under the sky. We are not told how its benefits are conferred. But how great is its operation!

How great is what is emblemed by Ch'ien! Strong, vigorous, undeflected, correct, and in all these qualities pure, unmixed, exquisite!

The six lines, as explained by the duke of Chou, bring forth and display its meaning, and everything about it is thus indirectly exhibited.

The great man at the proper time drives with these six dragons through the sky. The clouds move, and the rain is distributed; all under heaven enjoys repose.

In the superior man his conduct is the fruit of perfected virtue, which might be seen therefore in his daily course; but the force of that phrase, "lying hid," requires him to keep retired, and not yet show himself nor proceed to the full development of his course. While this is the case, the superior man knows that it is not the time for active doing.

The superior man learns and accumulates the results of his learning; puts questions, and discriminates among those results; dwells magnanimously and unambitiously in what he has attained to; and carries it into practice with benevolence. What the I says, "The dragon appears in the field: it will be advantageous to meet with the great man," has reference to the virtuous qualities of a ruler.

The great man is he who is in harmony, in his attributes, with heaven and earth; in his brightness, with the sun and moon; in his orderly procedure, with the four seasons; and in his relation to what is fortunate and what is calamitous, in harmony with the spirit-like operations of Providence. He may precede Heaven, and Heaven will not act in opposition to him; he may follow Heaven, but will act only as Heaven at the time would do. If Heaven will not act in opposition to him, how much less will men! How much less will the spirit-like operation of Providence!

The force of that phrase "exceeding the proper limits" indicates the knowing to advance but not to retire; to maintain but not to let perish; to get but not to lose.

He only is the sage who knows to advance and to retire, to maintain and to let perish; and that without ever acting incorrectly. Yes, he only is the sage!

K'UN

What is indicated by K'un is most gentle and weak

but, when put in motion, is hard and strong. It is most still, but is able to give every definite form.

"By following, it obtains its proper lord," and pursues its regular course.

It contains all things in itself, and its transforming power is glorious.

Yes, what docility marks the way of K'un! It receives the influences of heaven, and acts at the proper time.

The family that accumulates goodness is sure to have happiness in abundance, and the family that accumulates evil is sure to have misery in abundance. The murder of a ruler by his minister, or of his father by a son, is not the result of the events of one morning or one evening. The causes of it have generally accumulated, through the absence of early discrimination. The words of the I, "He treads on the hoarfrost; the strong ice will come by and by," show the natural issue and growth of things.

"Straight" indicates the correctness of the internal principle, and "square," the righteousness of the external act. The superior man thus represented, by his self-reverence maintains inward correctness, and in righteousness adjusts his external acts. His reverence and righteousness being thus established, his virtues are not solitary instances or of a single class. "Straight, square, and great, working his operations, without repeated efforts, in every respect advantageous": this shows how such a one has no doubts as to what he does.

Although the subject of this divided line, yin, has excellent qualities, he does not display them, but keeps them under restraint. "If he engage with them in the service of the king, and be successful, he will not claim that success for himself": this is the way of the earth, of a wife, of a minister. The way of the earth is "not to claim the merit of achievement," but on behalf of heaven to bring things to their proper issue.

Through the changes and transformations produced by heaven and earth, plants and trees grow luxuriantly. If the reciprocal influence of heaven and earth were shut up and restrained, we should have men of virtue and ability lying in obscurity. The words of the I, "A sack tied up: there will be no ground for blame or for praise," are in reality a lesson of caution.

The superior man emblemed here by the "yellow" and correct color, is possessed of comprehension and discrimination. He occupies the correct position of supremacy, but that emblem is on the lower part of his person. His excellence is in the center of his being, but it diffuses a complacency over his four limbs, and is manifested in his conduct of affairs: this is the perfection of excellence.

The subject of the yin or divided line thinking himself equal to the subject of the yang or undivided line, there is sure to be "a contest." As if indignant at there being no acknowledgment of the superiority of the subject of the yang line, the text uses the term "dragons." But still the subject of neither line can leave his class, and hence we have "the blood" mentioned. The mention of that as being both "azure and yellow" indicates the mixture of heaven and earth. Heaven's color is azure and earth's is yellow.

THE MASTER SAID

THE MASTER SAID

Further interpretations by Confucius of various hexagrams, extracted from the Fifth and Sixth Wings. They are gathered into numerical order for the convenience of the reader. (C.W.)

Hexagram 12, Line 5: "We see him who brings the distress and obstruction to a close, the great man and fortunate. But let him say 'We may perish! We may perish!' so shall the state of things become firm, as if bound to a clump of bushy mulberry trees."

The Master said:

"He who keeps danger in mind is he who will rest safe in his seat; he who keeps ruin in mind is he who will preserve his interests secure; he who sets the danger of disorder before him is he who will maintain the state of order. Therefore the superior man, when resting in safety, does not forget that danger may come; when in a state of security, he does not forget the possibility of ruin; and when all is in a state of order, he does not forget that disorder may come. Thus his person is kept safe, and his states and all their clans can be preserved. This is according to what the I says, 'Let him say, "Shall I perish? shall I perish?" so shall this state be firm, as if bound to a clump of bushy mulberry trees.'"

Hexagram 13, Line 5: "The representative of the union of men first cries out and weeps, and afterward laughs."

The Master said:

The ways of good men different seem.
This in a public office toils;
That in his home the time beguiles.
One man his lips with silence seals;
Another all his mind reveals.
But when two men are one in heart,
Not iron bolts keep them apart;
The words they in their union use,
Fragrance like orchid plants diffuse.

Hexagram 15, Line 3: "A superior man toiling laboriously and yet humble! He will bring things to an end, and with good fortune."

The Master said:

"He toils with success, but does not boast of it; he achieves merit, but takes no virtue to himself from it; this is the height of generous goodness, and speaks of the man who with great merit yet places himself below others. He wishes his virtue to be more and more complete, and in his intercourse with others to be more and more respectful; he who is so humble, carrying his respectfulness to the utmost, will be able to preserve himself in his position."

Hexagram 16, Line 2: ". . . one who is firm as a rock. He sees a thing without waiting till it has come to pass; with his firm correctness there will be good fortune."

The Master said:

"Does not he who knows the springs of things possess spirit-like wisdom? The superior man, in his intercourse with the high, uses no flattery, and, in his intercourse with the low, no coarse freedom: does not this show that he knows the springs of things? Those springs are the slight beginnings of movement, and the earliest indications of good fortune or ill. The superior man sees them, and acts accordingly without waiting for the delay of a single day. As is said in the I, 'He is firm as a rock, and acts without the delay of a single day. With firm goodness there will be good fortune.' Firm as a rock, how should he have to wait a single day to ensure his knowing those springs and his course? The superior man knows the minute and the manifested; he knows what is weak, and what is strong: he is a model to ten thousand."

Hexagram 21, Line 1: ". . . one with his feet in the stocks and deprived of his toes. There will be no error."

The Master said:

"The small man is not ashamed of what is not benevolent, nor does he fear to do what is not righteous. Without the prospect of gain he does not stimulate himself to what is good, nor does he correct himself without being moved. Self-correction, however, in what is small will make him careful in what would be of greater consequence; and this is the happiness of the small man. It is said in the I, 'His feet are in the stocks, and he is disabled in his toes: there will be no further occasion for blame.'"

Line 6: ". . . one wearing the cangue, and deprived of his ears. There will be evil."

The Master said:

"If acts of goodness be not accumulated, they are not sufficient to give its finish to one's name; if acts of evil be not accumulated, they are not sufficient to destroy one's life. The small man thinks that small acts of goodness are of no benefit, and does not do them; and that small deeds of evil do no harm, and does not abstain from them. Hence his wickedness becomes great till it cannot be covered, and his guilt becomes great till it cannot be pardoned. This is what the I says, 'He wears the cangue and his ears are destroyed: there will be evil.'"

Hexagram 24, Line 1: ". . . shows its subject returning from an error of no great extent, which would not proceed to anything requiring repentance. There will be great good fortune."

The Master said:

"I may venture to say that the son of the Yen family had nearly attained the standard of perfection. If anything that he did was not good, he was sure to become conscious of that; and when he knew it, he did not do the thing again. As is said in the I, 'The first line shows its subject returning from an error that has not led him far away. There is no occasion for repentance. There will be great good.'"

Hexagram 28, Line 1: ". . . shows its subject placing mats of the white grass beneath what he sets on the ground."

The Master said:

"To place the things on the ground might be considered sufficient; but when he places beneath them mats of the white grass, what occasion for blame can there be? Such a course shows the height of carefulness. The white grass is a trivial thing, but through the use made of it, it may become important. He who goes forward using such careful art will not fall into any error."

Hexagram 31, in general, from Line 4:

The Master said:

"In all the processes taking place under heaven, what is there of thinking? What is there of anxious scheming? They all come to the same successful issue, though by different paths; there is one result, though there might be a hundred anxious schemes. What is there of thinking? What is there of anxious scheming?"

Hexagram 40, Line 3:
The Master said:

"The makers of the I may be said to have known the philosophy of robbery. The I says, 'He is a burden-bearer, and yet rides in a carriage, thereby exciting robbers to attack him.' Burden-bearing is the business of a small man. A carriage is the vehicle of a gentleman. When a small man rides in the vehicle of a gentleman, robbers will think of taking it from him. When one is insolent to those above him, and oppressive to those below, robbers will wish to attack him. Careless laying up of things excites to robbery, as a woman's adorning of herself excites to lust. What the I says about the burden-bearer's riding in a carriage, and exciting robbers to attack him, shows how robbery is called out."

Line 6:
The Master said:

"The falcon is a bird of prey; the bow and arrow is a weapon of war; the shooter is a man. The superior man keeps his weapon concealed about his person, and waits for the proper time to move; doing this, how should his movement be other than successful? There is nothing to fetter or embarrass his movement; and hence, when he comes forth, he succeeds in his object. The language speaks of movement when the instrument necessary to it is ready and perfect."

Hexagram 41, Line 3:
The Master said:

"There is an intermingling of the genial influences of heaven and earth, and transformation in its various forms abundantly proceeds. There is an intercommunication of seed between male and female, and transformation in its living types proceeds. What is said in the I, 'Three individuals are walking together and one is made to disappear; there is but one man walking, and he gets his mate,' tells us of the effort in nature at oneness of operation."

Hexagram 42, Line 5: ". . . shows its subject with sincere heart seeking to benefit all below. There need be no question about it; the result will be great good fortune. All below will with sincere heart acknowledge his goodness.

The Master said:

"The superior man in a high place composes himself before he tries to move others; makes his mind restful and easy before he speaks; settles the principles of his intercourse with others before he seeks anything from them. The superior man cultivates these three things, and so is complete. If he try to move others while he is himself in unrest, the people will not act with him; if he speak while he is himself in a state of apprehension, the people will not respond to him; if without certain principles of intercommunication, he issue his requests, the people will not grant them. When there are none to accord with him, those who work to injure him will make their appearance. As is said in the I, 'We see one to whose advantage none will contribute, while some will seek to assail him. He observes no regular rule in the ordering of his heart: there will be evil.'"

Hexagram 47, Line 3: "It is said in the I, 'The third line shows its subject distressed before a rock, and trying to lay hold of thorns; entering into his palace and not seeing his wife: there will be evil.'"

The Master said:

"If one be distressed by what need not distress him, his name is sure to be disgraced; if he lay hold on what he should not touch, his life is sure to be imperiled. In disgrace and danger, his death will soon come; is it possible for him in such circumstances to see his wife?"

Hexagram 50, Line 4: ". . . shows the cauldron with its feet broken, and its contents overturned and spilled. Its subject will be made to blush."

The Master said:

"Virtue small and office high; wisdom small and plans great; strength small and burden heavy: where such conditions exist, it is seldom that they do not end in evil. As is said in the I, 'The tripod's feet are overthrown, and the ruler's food is overturned. The body of him who is thus indicated is wet with shame: there will be evil.'"

Hexagram 60, Line 1: "He does not quit the courtyard before his door; there will be no occasion for blame."

The Master said:

"When disorder arises, it will be found that ill-advised

speech was the stepping-stone to it. If a ruler do not keep secret his deliberations with his minister, he will lose that minister. If a minister do not keep secret his deliberations with his ruler, he will lose his life. If important matters in the germ be not kept secret, that will be injurious to their accomplishment. Therefore the superior man is careful to maintain secrecy, and does not allow himself to speak."

Hexagram 61, Line 2:

> Here hid, retired, cries out the crane;
> Her young's responsive cry sounds there.
> Of spirits good I drain this cup;
> With thee a cup I'll freely share.

The Master said:

"The superior man occupies his apartment and sends forth his words. If they be good, they will be responded to at a distance of more than a thousand li; how much more will they be so in the nearer circle! He occupies his apartment and sends forth his words. If they be evil, they will awaken opposition at a distance of more than a thousand li; how much more will they do so in the nearer circle! Words issue from one's person, and proceed to affect the people. Actions proceed from what is near, and their effects are seen at a distance. Words and actions are the hinge and spring of the superior man. The movement of that hinge and spring determines glory or disgrace. His words and actions move heaven and earth; may he be careless in regard to them?"

The Master said:

"Is not the I a perfect book? . . . It was by the I

that the sages exalted their virtue, and enlarged their sphere of occupation. Their wisdom was high, and their rules of conduct were solid. That loftiness was after the pattern of heaven; that solidity, after the pattern of earth. Heaven and earth having their positions as assigned to them, the changes of nature take place between them. The nature of man having been completed, and being continually preserved, it is the gate of all good courses and righteousness."

THE SHIH HEXAGRAM

interpreted by James Legge

An interpretation of *Shih* by James Legge; from Translator's Introduction to the original edition. (C.W.)

To illustrate what I have said on the subject matter of the I by example: It shall be the treatment of the seventh hexagram which king Wen named Shih, meaning Hosts. The character is also explained as meaning "multitudes"; and in fact, in a feudal kingdom, the multitudes of the people were all liable to become its army, when occasion required, and the "host" and the "population" might be interchangeable terms. As Froude expresses it in the introductory chapter to his *History of England,* "Every man was regimented somewhere."

The hexagram Shih is composed of the two trigrams K'an and K'un, exhibiting waters collected on the earth; and in other symbolisms besides that of the I, waters indicate assembled multitudes of men. The waters on which the mystical Babylon sits in the Apocalypse are explained as "peoples and multitudes and nations and tongues." I do not positively affirm that it was by this interpretation of the trigrams that king Wen saw in Shih the feudal hosts of his country collected, for neither from him nor his son do we learn, by their direct affirmation, that they had any acquaintance with the trigrams of Fu Hsi. The name which he gave the figure shows, however, that he saw in it the feudal hosts in the field. How shall their expedition be conducted that it may come to a successful issue?

Looking again at the figure, we see that it is made

up of five yin lines, and of one yang. The yang line occupies the central place in the lower trigram, the most important place, next to the fifth, in the whole hexagram. It will represent, in the language of the commentators, "the lord of the whole figure"; and the parties represented by other lines may be expected to be of one mind with him or obedient to him. He must be the leader of the hosts. If he were on high, in the fifth place, he would be the sovereign of the kingdom. This is what king Wen says:

"Shih indicates how in the case which it supposes, with firmness and correctness, and a leader of age and experience, there will be good fortune and no error."

This is a good auspice. Let us see how the duke of Chou expands it. He says:

"The first line, yin, shows the host going forth according to the rules for such a movement. If those rules be not good, there will be evil."

We are not told what the rules for a military expedition were. Some commentators understand them of the reasons justifying the movement, that it should be to repress and punish disorder and rebellion. Others, with more likelihood, take them to be the discipline or rules laid down to be observed by the troops. The line is yin in a yang place, "not correct": this justifies the caution given in the duke's second sentence.

The Text goes on:

"The second line, yang, shows the leader in the midst of the hosts. There will be good fortune and no error. The king has thrice conveyed to him his charge."

This does not need any amplification. The duke saw in the yang line the symbol of the leader, who enjoyed the full confidence of his sovereign, and whose authority admitted of no opposition.

On the third line it is said:

"The third line, yin, shows how the hosts may possibly have many commanders: in such a case there will be evil."

The third place is odd, and should be occupied by a yang line, instead of which we have a yin line in it. But it is at the top of the lower trigram, and its subject should be in office or activity. There is suggested the idea that its subject has vaulted over the second line, and wishes to share in the command and honor of him who has been appointed sole commander-in-chief. The lesson in the previous line is made of none effect. We have a divided authority in the expedition. The result can only be evil.

On the fourth line the duke wrote:

"The fourth line, yin, shows the hosts in retreat: there is no error."

The line is also weak, and victory cannot be expected; but in the fourth place a yin line is in its correct position, and its subject will do what is right in his circumstances. He will retreat, and a retreat is for him the part of wisdom. When safely effected, where advance would be disastrous, a retreat is as glorious as victory.

Under the fifth line we read:

"The fifth line, yin, shows birds in the fields which it is advantageous to seize and destroy. There will be no error. If the oldest son lead the host, and younger men be also in command, however firm and correct he may be, there will be evil."

We have an intimation in this passage that only defensive war, or war waged by the rightful authority to put down rebellion and lawlessness, is right. The "birds in the fields" are emblematic of plunderers and invaders, whom it will be well to destroy. The fifth line symbolizes the chief authority, but here he is weak or humble, and has given all power and authority to execute judgment into the hands of the commander-in-chief, who is the oldest son; and in the subject of line 3 we have an example of the younger men who would cause evil if allowed to share his power.

Finally, on the sixth line the duke wrote:

"The topmost line, yin, shows the great ruler delivering his charges to the men who have distinguished themselves, appointing some to be rulers of states, and others to be chiefs of clans. But small men should not be employed in such positions."

The action of the hexagram has been gone through. The expedition has been conducted to a successful end. The enemy has been subdued. His territories are at the disposal of the conqueror. The commander-in-chief has done his part well. His sovereign, "the great ruler," comes upon the scene, and rewards the officers who have been conspicuous by their bravery and skill, conferring on them rank and lands. But he is warned to have respect in doing so to their moral character. Small men, of ordinary or less than ordinary character, may be rewarded with riches and certain honors; but land and the welfare of its population should not be given into the hands of any who are not equal to the responsibility of such a trust.

The above is a specimen of what I have called the essays that make up the I of Chou. So would king Wen and his son have had all military expeditions conducted in their country three thousand years ago. It seems to me that the principles which they lay down might find a suitable application in the modern warfare of our civilized and Christian Europe. The inculcation of such lessons cannot have been without good effect in China during the long course of its history.

Shih is a fair specimen of its class. From the other 63 hexagrams lessons are deduced, for the most part equally good and striking. But why, it may be asked, why should they be conveyed to us by such an array of lineal figures, and in such a farrago of emblematic representations? It is not for the foreigner to insist on such a question. The Chinese have not valued them the less because of the antiquated dress in which their lessons are arrayed. Hundreds of their commentators have evolved and developed their meaning with a minuteness of detail and felicity of illustration that leave nothing to be desired. It is for foreign students of Chinese to gird up their loins for the mastery of the book instead of talking about it as mysterious and all but inexplicable.

THE *I Ching* AS A BOOK OF DIVINATION

_____

The *I Ching* as a Book of Divination

. . . divination was practiced in China from a very early time. I will not say 5,200 years ago, in the days of Fu Hsi, for I cannot repress doubts of his historical personality; but as soon as we tread the borders of something like credible history, we find it existing. In the *Shu Ching,* in a document that purports to be of the twenty-third century B.C., divination by means of the tortoise shell is mentioned; and somewhat later we find that method continuing, and also divination by the lineal figures, manipulated by means of the stalks of a plant . . . which is still cultivated on and about the grave of Confucius, where I have myself seen it growing.

—James Legge,
I Ching.

THE *I Ching* AS A BOOK OF DIVINATION

The Chinese word most commonly associated with divination is *kua*. It became so closely linked to the *I Ching* that it also symbols *the diagrams*. The primitive character derives from components that combine "earth that produces all things" with the symbol for the tortoise shell.

It is vain to expect that we can visualize with any certainty the early divination practices, to know all the symbols connected with it, or even to know precisely the meanings of the different characters still associated with divining. *Chan* is another Chinese word for divination, and means to ask about some enterprise by means of the tortoise shell. *Shih* means to divine with stems of the milfoil. *Chi* means to divine by a pencil. *Wai* is divination concerning a dream. In the Chinese language ideas flow and mix, characters used as nouns can also be used as verbs or other parts of speech, context tinctures meaning. This leads to nuances in talking and telepathy in reading. And the classical style of written Chinese is terse in the extreme, and highly symbolic. The characters are not words; they represent generalizations rather than particulars.

Entrapped as we Westerners are within the bonds of ororverbalized communication, can we presume to be arbitrary and declare either *this* rendering to be correct, or *that* rendering?

Yet we must dare to believe we perceive. We must dare to expand our symbols. We must in the darkness which is yin, be responsive to light, which is yang. We must follow Legge in his leap from "mind to mind"—opening our consciousness to the experience of the symbol even when our minds cannot articulate it.

Confucius gives a precedent for this:

> " 'The written characters are not the full exponent of speech, and speech is not the full expression of ideas;—is it impossible then to discover the ideas of the sages? . . . The sages made their emblematic symbols to set forth fully their ideas; appointed all the diagrams to show fully the truth and falsehood of things; appended their explanations to give the full expression of their words; and changed the various lines and made general the method of doing so, to exhibit fully what was advantageous. They thus stimulated the people as by drums and dances, thereby completely developing the spirit-like character of the I.' "

When looking up *divining* in an English language dictionary one is struck by the great number of meanings that have attached themselves to this word. Looking up its root in a Latin dictionary, one is struck by the strong association of *numena* with every Latin connotation. Similarly, to the Chinese sages divination probably had larger meanings than prognostication.

The first divining from the shell of the tortoise was apparently by observing the cracks in their natural form. Later, the shell was singed, and the lines which resulted from this heating were studied to select the appropriate hexagram. Later, as stated in the *I*, we are told about manipulating the milfoil stalks. This is a lengthy, complicated method employing arithmetic formulae. A modern transposition to coins instead of the stalks, but retaining the arithmetic system, is also in use. Both these methods require study, preparation, and skill. They are concerned with divining as prognostication.

What is the true nature of the oracle contained within the *I Ching*? Is it a means of precognition concerning the external world? Is it the ability to read the curve of the future when we quiet our thoughts, examine the past, and analyze the present?

Or, if we approach the *I* with receptive minds and our senses attuned to oracular revelation, do we make contact with cosmic consciousness? Perhaps the *I* puts us in touch with our own disguised, instinctive, drives. Under quiet circumstances, is it possible to connect the conscious mind with its unconscious, to explore the dark side of the psyche? Or do we, merely by emptying our minds of raggle-taggle thoughts, tap nourishment from the universal rhizome?

If any of these speculations approach what the sages meant by prognostication, then the method used in divining is in itself a symbolic act. And it would then follow that any carefully planned, consistently practiced, method would yield the same results as the complicated method of the stalks.

To know the *I Ching* we should experience it as a book of divination. We can no more approach the *I*'s source of wisdom without trying our hand at divining than we can know the sound of a piano without a key striking. The following method* is offered as a short-

---

*This method was developed by Carrie Jespersen Sinnott from a series of experiments in parapsychology. It is given here with her gracious permission.

ened, modern version. The basic concept is that, in forming the lines, there must be a choice possible: the line must always have the possibility of being either yang or yin, with the option for this not controlled by the conscious mind.

1) Use twelve identical, small objects—metal coins, plastic slugs; any identical tokens will do.

2) Six of these must be bright, polished or light colored, to represent yang, or undivided, lines.

3) Six must be dull, or dark colored, to represent the yin, or divided, lines.

4) An inquiry must be formed within the mind. This requires the setting aside of distractions, and the clarification of the question. To ask a fuzzy question is to receive a fuzzy answer. Furthermore, one must have exhausted all avenues of arriving at an answer through his conscious, rational thinking.

5) When the inquiry has been formulated, the structure of hexagrams must be kept firmly in the mind: line one is always the bottom line, line six the upper, and lines two through five take their appropriate places between.

6) "In all these operations forming the I, there is no thought and no action." That is, without knowledge of which color token is drawn from whatever receptacle is used, six are taken at random, one after another, from among the twelve. They are placed before the consulter in ascending order, lines one through six.

If one has placed first a light token (yang), then three dark tokens (yin), followed by two light (yang) on topmost lines five and six, the consulter has symbolized the trigram of Chen, Thunder, with that of Sun, Wind, above.

This can be translated to paper as a figure: Line 1, the lowest, is undivided and has three divided lines above; the topmost lines, five and six, are undivided.

Either using the Hexagram Locater, or in the Alphabetical Reference Table under Chen, one notes that Chen as the lower trigram (with which the action begins), with Sun above is Hexagram 42: I.

7) One then turns to Hexagram 42 and reads what is contained beneath its symbol. Through his own personal idiom the diviner must transpose the explanations and symbols of an ancient, feudal society into the symbols of his own environment and era—and thus constitute the answer to his twentieth century question.

In the Book of Changes we read:

". . . all events possible under the sky . . . have their representation.

"The diagrams make manifest by their appended explanations, the ways of good and ill fortune, and show virtuous actions in their spiritual relations. In this way, by consulting them, we may receive an answer to our doubts, and we may also by means of them assist the spiritual power in its agency in nature and providence.

"The operations forming the I are the method by which the sages searched out exhaustively what was deep and investigated the minutest springs of things . . . therefore they could make speed without hurry, and reached their destination without traveling.

"The most thorough mastery of all the complex phenomena under the sky is obtained from the diagrams. The greatest stimulus to movement in adaptation to all affairs under the sky is obtained from the explanations."

Another way to participate in the oracle-wisdom of the I is by lineal consideration. That is, to look at the lines, and without recourse to words, draw conclusions or resolve doubts. This is not without precedent. Wang Pi, one of the great commentators of the I, found much wisdom in the I by the reading of the words without reference to the lines. He also found much to be gained by contemplation of the lines without reference to words.

The action of the hexagram begins with that of the lower trigram. The lines are numbered one through six beginning with the bottom, or inner, line and ascending to the sixth, or outer line. Harmony is strengthened when each line is occupied by the appropriate symbol: odd places by yang, or undivided lines, and even places by yin, or divided lines:

```
6.  - -
5.  —
4.  - -
3.  —
2.  - -
1.  —
```

The reason for this is that a yang line is made with one stroke, hence designated odd; a yin line is made with two strokes, hence designated even.

Another indication of good auspice is correlation, which consists of a combination of one yang with one yin line, as opposed to lines in correlation being both yang, or both yin. When yang and yin combine in this way, the correlation is said to be "complete."

Correlates:

> line 1 is the correlate of line 4;
> line 2 is the correlate of line 5;
> line 3 is the correlate of line 6;
> line 4 is the correlate of line 1;
> line 5 is the correlate of line 2;
> line 6 is the correlate of line 3.

Correlation of lines 2 and 5 have peculiar value and force. When line 2 is yin and line 5 is yang, the correlation is not only "complete," it has added significance:

> 6.
> 5. —
> 4.
> 3.
> 2. - -
> 1.

Line 5 is called the "lord of the whole figure." Line 2 is of second importance. These "central" places, lines 2 and 5, are the middle lines in upper and lower trigrams forming a hexagram. Some users of the *I*, who have developed a strong body of thought relative to the eight trigrams, interpret a hexagram solely by reading the trigrams, applying the general concepts, and their own intuition.

By remaining alert to the influences of the interrelationship of the lines, a deeper meaning can be read into the explanations.

When the lines are not in their appropriate places, a careful reading of THE TEXT will usually advise the subject how to counteract the influence. Compare Chi Chi, number 63, with Wei Chi, number 64:

CHI CHI:	WEI CHI:
6. - -	6. —
5. —	5. - -
4. - -	4. —
3. —	3. - -
2. - -	2. —
1. —	1. - -

CHI CHI:	WEI CHI:
lines in proper places	lines in inappropriate places

CHI CHI:	WEI CHI:
6. yin	6. yang
5. yang	5. yin
4. yin	4. yang
3. yang	3. yin
2. yin	2. yang
1. yang	1. yin

CHI CHI:	WEI CHI:
conveys success and completion	indicates there is much to be done still

See the complete explanations given at Hexagram 63, Chi Chi, and Hexagram 64, Wei Chi.

It is also possible to use Fu Hsi's trigrams in a thoroughly modern way: following but not imitating king Wen. The eight symbols then serve as shortcuts to programming the mind, factoring into our image psychology the potential most needed. In such a case, to apply what might be called cybernetic philosophy, we could consider:

CH'IEN, the time for action.

TUI, a time for rest and relaxation.

LI, time for human relationships.

CHEN, time for change and revolution; acting out.

K'UN, time for renewal, psychological hibernation.

KEN, meditation, examination of the inward mind.

K'AN, a time to venture and course ahead.

SUN, persuasion through the expression of ideas.

And it is entirely possible that by reading the *I* as a book of wisdom the symbols of the trigrams will assume an entirely personal potential. For some they will become dynamic concepts which—when held firmly in the mind revolving on the axis of deep desire before the vision of the inner eye—profoundly affect the future course of events because they have profoundly affected the individual who will take part in these events.

In such a case one has not only learned to use the Changes of Tao, one *is* Changes—with all the creative joy, intelligent stirring, receptive meditation and coursing persuasion with which the ancient sages encompassed the myriads of things.

Is this the substance of the *I Ching,* or is there more to it, something that lies beyond?

"Anciently, when the sages made the I, in order to give mysterious assistance to the spiritual Intelligences, they produced the rules for the use of the divining plant . . . when the sages made the I, it was with the design that its figures should be in conformity with the principles underlying the natures of men and things, and the ordinances for them appointed by Heaven ..."

What is this "mysterious assistance," "the principles underlying the natures of men and things," and the "ordinances for them appointed by Heaven"?

If these concepts embraced prognostication alone, is it likely that Confucius, at an advanced age, would have said that, if given some years added to his life, he would spend fifty of them in the study of the *I*?

If Legge is right that the part of the *I* called THE TEXT is the oldest section of this work, then the section dealing with the origin and invention of the trigrams must have had an oral tradition which predated the written text. And if this is so, then its nature will have to be deduced by indirection and internal evidence, however scant.

What we must divine is "the secret principle." Confucius said: "The trigrams Ch'ien and K'un may be regarded as the gate of the I." The secret principle, not being delineated, must lie beyond that gate. Beyond words, that is, in the area of thought unshackled.

Today passing through that gate can be accomplished instantly, by means of drugs and chemicals. Ch'ien is analogous to a door opened, and K'un to a door closed. The *I* implies a control of these doors.

This is mind penetrating itself. This is a journey to the other side of the psyche. But the psychedelic world of the sages was entered with a discipline. They used the mind as a power, and never surrendered control of it. They learned the principle of the *I* that was in accord with heaven and earth, and saw the course of things "without rent or confusion."

As *kua* is a mysterious word of many associations, so have we a root word of many derivatives: *cept,* from the Latin "capere," to lay hold of. The power of mind is its thought, and the irreducible state of thought is the *cept.* The power of mind, in its diminished state, is *ceptive* and in its replenished state, can lay hold of Fu Hsi's "myriads of things." This is displayed in our symbols of con*cept,* per*cept*ion, in*cept*ion, pre*cept*— the function of the mind can swivel full circle from the root word; cepts can be used as the sages used the diagrams: to comprehend all things. Through the cept we influence the course of things, enter into the work of the world. Through ception, and by cepting, we can join creation itself, stand near Sheng Ti and participate in the endless changes of the tao.

If this can be accepted, then we can see the trigrams as a kind of psychedelic shorthand which directs us to the power of "the secret principle" of the *I.* And when we divine the future it is because we are taking part in shaping it.

Far from being fanciful, this is in accord with psychological truth: by the use of intellect we introject a force into the course of everyday occurrences which has effect. Though the full scope of the effect may lie beyond our cognition, this does not deny its effectiveness. It is analogous to the fact that in order to construct a table one must first constellate within the mind an image of a table: a surface resting upon supports.

This is part of a principle we Westerners are not in the habit of using consciously. When we can once more, as we have many times in the past, expand our conscious minds to incorporate a new function, we will become receptive to our next step in human progress. Whether we call this principle tao, cause and effect,

Jungian synchronicity, evolution, God, logic, or even horse sense, is relatively unimportant. A label is not the thing itself. The thing itself has its own signification regardless of the name we give it.

In this shrinking and crowded world mutual understanding is destined to be the ultimate means of survival. Before we can make the best use of our technology, we must first learn the art of aggressive respect. We must develop the ability to become perceptive of the unique human accomplishments which lie outside the physical sciences. We must respect every being and his human endeavor without prejudice. And we must develop a combining sense that venerates the whole body of man's mental progress without presuming to make value judgments regarding its separate parts.

It is here that the *I Ching* becomes a book of wisdom not Chinese but human, no longer a storehouse of occulted mysteries but a rationale.

That the *I* has been used as mere fortune-telling, and often by charlatans, does not diminish its worth. The mathematical truths discovered by Girolamo Cardano (Italy; 1501-1576) are no less truths because they first appeared in the handbook for gamblers written by this vain, lying, greedy, obscene and yet brilliant Renaissance rascal. His extraordinary theories of probabilities have enriched the science of pure mathematics, though the use he made of them did not.

Both implicit and explicit in the *I Ching* is such truth. That we are not habituated to its conceptual method, or that priestly obscurants have manipulated this wisdom for their personal gain does not affect its content. It is for us, now, to avail ourselves of all we can make use of.

The world will not stand still while we improve it.

Or even while we examine it. That is what the *Book of Changes* is all about: by accepting as our natural condition a state of flux we can learn to act positively, with the forces of the cosmos and not against them. Within the wisdom of the *I* is an axis that turns on a center in all directions, pivoting spherically. It is in accord with this principle that the *I*'s unique process, offering a different polarity to each individual, functions.

If this cannot be accepted, then one must search further for the principle.

The sages did not proselytize. The *I* was learned, not taught. The Chinese were a practical people. Their perception told them the course of things, and they moved with that course. If the auspices were wrong, if the time was evil, they symboled Ken: they rested in the quietude of a mountain, they arrested the inauspicious course with the immovable mass of a mountain. They contemplated until Ch'ien originated a new course, and K'un brought forth its substance.

"The eight trigrams served to determine good and evil issues of events, and from this determination was produced the successful prosecution of the great business of life."

The yin of our minds cannot be penetrated except by our own yang. We make this journey alone, and there are no words to describe it. But its effect is told in the *I*:

"When the looper coils itself up, it thereby straightens itself again . . . when we minutely investigate the nature and reasons of things, till we have entered into the inscrutable and spirit-like in them, we attain to the largest practical application of them; when that application becomes the quickest and readiest, and all personal restfulness is secured, our virtue is thereby exalted.

"Going on beyond this, we reach a point which it is hardly possible to know. We have thoroughly comprehended the inscrutable and spirit-like, and know the processes of transformation—this is the fullness of virtue."

—Clae Waltham

THE HEXAGRAMS

THE HEXAGRAMS

A learner will consider what is said under the diagrams, and then speak; he will deliberate on what is said in the explanations of the lines, and then move. By such considerations and deliberations he will be able to make all the changes which he undertakes successful.

—James Legge,
I Ching.

The Hexagrams

Heaven is lofty and honorable; earth is low. Their symbols, Ch'ien and K'un, with their respective meanings, were determined in accordance with this.

Things low and high appear displayed in a similar relation. The upper and lower trigrams, and the relative position of individual lines, had their places assigned accordingly.

Movement and rest are the regular qualities of their respective subjects. Hence comes the definite distinction of the several lines as the yang and yin.

Affairs are arranged together according to their tendencies, and things are divided according to their classes. Hence were produced the interpretations in the I concerning what is good (or lucky) and evil (or unlucky).

In the heavens there are the different figures there completed, and on the earth there are the different bodies there formed. Corresponding to them were the changes and transformations exhibited in the I.

After this fashion a yang and a yin line were manipulated together till there were the eight trigrams, and those eight trigrams were added, each to itself and to all the others, till the sixty-four hexagrams were formed.

Thus the sage surveyed all the complex phenomena under the sky. He then considered in his mind how they could be figured, and by means of the diagrams represented their material forms and their character.

A later sage was able to survey the motive influences working all under the sky. He contemplated them in their common action and special nature, in order to bring out the standard and proper tendency of each. He then appended his explanation to each line to determine the good or evil indicated by it.

We have the exciting forces of thunder and lighting; the fertilizing influences of wind and rain; and the revolutions of the sun and moon, which give rise to cold and warmth.

The attributes expressed by Ch'ien constitute the male; those expressed by K'un constitute the female. Ch'ien symbolizes Heaven, which directs the great beginnings of things; K'un symbolizes Earth, which gives to them their completion. It is by the ease with which it proceeds that Ch'ien directs as it does, and by its unhesitating response that K'un exhibits such ability.

He who attains to this ease of Heaven will be easily understood, and he who attains to this freedom from laborious effort of the Earth will be easily followed. He who is easily understood will have adherents, and he who is easily followed will achieve success. He who has adherents can continue long, and he who achieves success can become great. To be able to continue long shows the virtue of the wise and able man; to be able to become great is the heritage he will acquire.

With the attainment of such ease and such freedom from laborious effort, the mastery is got of all principles under the sky. With the attainment of that mastery, the sage makes good his position in the middle between heaven and earth. (J.L.)

What appears below each hexagram under the heading THE TEXT is the oldest writing in the development and explanation of the 64 hexagrams, dating from the 12th century B.C.

The first paragraph refers to the hexagrams as a whole, and is often referred to as the T'uan. It is attributed to king Wen.

Legge allows himself one of his few leaps of imagination as, in his introduction, he says:

> I like to think of king Wen when incarcerated in Lu-li with the 64 figures arranged before him. Each hexagram assumed a mystic meaning, and glowed with a deep significance. He made it tell him of the qualities of various objects of nature, or of the principles of human society, or of the condition, actual and possible, of the kingdom. He named the figures, each by a term descriptive of the idea with which he had connected it in his mind, and then he proceeded to set that idea forth, now with a note of exhortation, now with a note of warning.

Elsewhere, Legge advises us that when the T'uan says "in the case which it supposes," or "presupposes," that king Wen makes reference to a particular situation and that the modern reader should not be too literal in the details of interpreting it.

The explanations numbered 1 through 6 are attributed to king Wen's son, the duke of Chou. They are called the Yao.

What appears under the heading FROM THE WINGS is a later writing, gathered from the first three wings, and if they are indeed the work of Confucius they represent comments on the I between six and seven centuries later. What is more likely is that they represent a synthesis from many centuries and many scholars, and have gathered themselves together as the result of centuries of winnowing and editing, additions, losses and mutilations, and interpolations.

What appears under the heading FROM THE NOTES OF JAMES LEGGE is only a small selection from the exhaustive and compendious deliberations of an aroused scholar who was also a sleeping poet. (C.W.)

PLATE I

PLATE I.
The Hexagrams, in the order in which they appear in the I, and were arranged by king Wên.

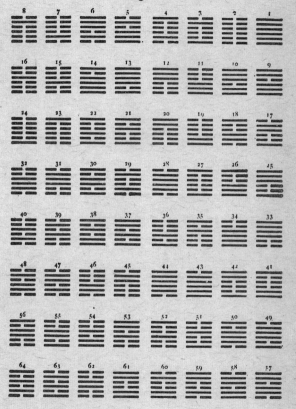

Note that the numbering moves from right to left, as proper in China.

CH'IEN, HEAVEN
Repeated

1 CH'IEN, HEAVEN

THE TEXT:

Ch'ien represents what is great and originating, penetrating, advantageous, correct and firm.

1. In the first line, yang, we see its subject as the dragon lying hid in the deep; it is not the time for active doing.

2. In the second line, yang, we see its subject as the dragon appearing in the field. It will be advantageous to meet with the great man.

3. In the third line, yang, we see its subject as the superior man active and vigilant all the day, and in the evening, still careful and apprehensive. The position is dangerous, but there will be no mistake.

4. In the fourth line, yang, we see its subject as the dragon looking as if he were leaping up, but still in the deep. There will be no mistake.

5. In the fifth line, yang, we see its subject as the dragon on the wing in the sky. It will be advantageous to meet with the great man.

6. In the sixth line, yang, we see its subject as the dragon exceeding the proper limits. There will be occasion for repentance.

If the host of dragons were to divest themselves of their heads, there would be good fortune.

FROM THE WINGS:

Vast is the great and originating power indicated by Ch'ien! All things owe to it their beginning. It contains all the meaning belonging to the name of heaven. The clouds move and the rain is distributed; the various things appear in their developed forms.

The sages grandly understand the connection between the end and the beginning, and how the indications of the six lines are accomplished each in its season. Accordingly, they mount the carriage drawn by those six dragons at the proper times, and drive through the sky.

The method of Ch'ien is to change and transform, so that everything obtains its correct nature as appointed by the mind of heaven. Thereafter conditions of great harmony are preserved in union. The result is "what is advantageous, and correct and firm."

The sage appears aloft, high above all things, and the myriad states all enjoy repose.

Heaven, in its motion, gives the idea of strength. The superior man, in accordance with this, nerves himself to ceaseless activity.

1. "The dragon lies hid in the deep; it is not the time for active doing": this appears from the strong yang line in the lowest place.

2. "The dragon appears in the field": the diffusion of virtuous influence has been wide.

3. "Active and vigilant all the day": this refers to the treading of the proper path over and over again.

4. "He seems to be leaping up, but is still in the deep": if he advance, there will be no error.

5. "The dragon is on the wing in the sky": the great man rouses himself to his work.

6. "The dragon exceeds the proper limits; there will be occasion for repentance": a state of fullness that should not be indulged in long.

FROM THE NOTES OF JAMES LEGGE:

The "connection between the end and the beginning" is that of cause and effect in the operations of nature and the course of human affairs. The various steps in that course are symbolized by the lines of the hexagram. The ideal sage, conducting his ideal government, taking his measures accordingly, is represented as driving through the sky in a carriage drawn by six dragons.

The motion of heaven is a complete revolution every day, resumed again the next. So moves "the unwearied sun from day to day," making it a good symbol of renewed, untiring effort.

K'UN, EARTH
Repeated

2 K'un; Earth

THE TEXT:

K'un represents what is great and originating, penetrating, advantageous, correct and having the firmness of a mare. When the superior man, here intended, has to make any movement he will go astray if he take the initiative; if he follow, he will find his proper lord. The advantageousness will be seen in his getting friends in the southwest, and losing friends in the northeast. If he rest in correctness and firmness, there will be good fortune.

1. In the first line, yin, we see its subject treading on hoarfrost. The strong ice will come by and by.

2. The second line, yin, shows the attribute of being straight, square, and great. Its operation, without repeated efforts, will be in every respect advantageous.

3. The third line, yin, shows its subject keeping his excellence under restraint, but firmly maintaining it. If he should have occasion to engage in the king's service, though he will not claim the success for himself, he will bring affairs to a good issue.

4. The fourth line, yin, shows the symbol of a sack tied up. There will be no ground for blame or for praise.

5. The fifth line, yin, shows the yellow lower garment. There will be great good fortune.

6. The sixth line, yin, shows dragons fighting in the wild. Their blood is purple and yellow.

The lines of this hexagram are all yin. If those who are thus represented be perpetually correct and firm, advantage will arise.

FROM THE WINGS:

Complete is the "great and originating capacity" indicated by K'un! All things owe to it their birth; it receives obediently the influences of Heaven.

K'un, in its largeness, supports and contains all things. Its excellent capacity matches the unlimited power of Ch'ien. Its comprehension is wide, and its brightness great. The various things obtain by it their full development.

The mare is a creature of earthly kind. Its power of moving on the earth is without limit; it is mild and docile, advantageous and firm. Such is the course of the superior man.

"If he take the initiative, he goes astray": he misses his proper course. "If he follow," he is docile, and gets into his regular course. "In the southwest he will get friends": he will be walking with those of his own class. "In the northeast he will lose friends": but in the end there will be ground for congratulation.

"The good fortune arising from resting in firmness" corresponds to the unlimited capacity of the earth.

The capacity and sustaining power of the earth is what is denoted by K'un. The superior man, in accordance with this, with his large virtue supports men and things.

1. "He is treading on hoarfrost; the strong ice will come by and by": the cold air has begun to take form. Allow it to go on quietly according to its nature, and the hoarfrost will come to strong ice.

2. The movement indicated by the second line, yin, is "from the straight line to the square." "Its operation, without repeated effort, in every way advantageous," shows the brilliant result of the way of earth.

3. "He keeps his excellence under restraint, but firmly maintains it": at the proper time he will manifest it. "He may have occasion to engage in the king's service": great is the glory of his wisdom.

4. "A sack tied up; there will be no error": this shows how, through carefulness, no injury will be received.

5. "The yellow lower-garment; there will be great good fortune": this follows from that ornamental color being in the right and central place.

6. "The dragons fight in the wild": the onward course indicated by K'un is pursued to extremity.

Those who are thus represented becoming perpetually correct and firm, there will thereby be a great consummation.

FROM THE NOTES OF JAMES LEGGE:

The same attributes are ascribed to K'un as to Ch'ien; but with a difference. The figure, made up of six yin lines, expresses the ideal of subordination and docility. The superior man, represented by it, must not take the initiative. By following he will find his lord.

Line 2 presents the earth according to the Chinese conception: as a great cube.

Line 6: "In the wild" has the meaning of "beyond proper limits" of Hexagram 1. "Their blood is purple and yellow": the color proper to heaven cr the sky, and the color proper to earth.

The "penetrating" or developing ability of K'un is displayed in the processes of growth. "The brightness" refers to the beauty that shines forth in the vegetable and animal kingdoms.

"Resting in firmness" is the normal course of K'un. Where it is pursued, the good effect will be great, great as the unlimited capacity of the earth.

Ch'ien originates. K'un produces.

K'AN, WATER
over
CHEN, THUNDER

3 CHUN; STRUGGLE

THE TEXT:

Chun indicates that in the case which it presupposes there will be great progress and success, and the advantage will come from being correct and firm. But any movement in advance should not be lightly undertaken. There will be advantage in appointing feudal princes.

1. The first line, yang, shows the difficulty its subject has in advancing. It will be advantageous for him to abide correct and firm; advantageous also to be made a feudal ruler.

2. The second line, yin, shows its subject distressed and obliged to return; even the horses of her chariot also seem to be retreating. But not by a spoiler is she assailed, but by one who seeks her to be his wife. The young lady maintains her firm correctness, and declines a union. After ten years she will be united, and have children.

3. The third line, yin, shows one following the deer without the guidance of the forester, and only finding himself in the midst of the forest. The superior man, acquainted with the secret risks, thinks it better to give up the chase. If he went forward, he would regret it.

4. The fourth line, yin, shows its subject as a lady, the horses of whose chariot appear in retreat. She seeks,

however, the help of him who seeks her to be his wife. Advance will be fortunate; all will turn out advantageously.

5. The fifth line, yang, shows the difficulties in the way of its subject's dispensing the rich favors that might be expected from him. With firmness and correctness there will be good fortune in small things; even with them in great things there will be evil.

6. The topmost line, yin, shows its subject with the horses of his chariot obliged to retreat, and weeping tears of blood in streams.

FROM THE WINGS:

In Chun we have the yang Ch'ien and the yin K'un commencing their intercourse, and difficulties arising. Movement in the midst of peril gives rise to "great progress and success, through firm correctness." By the action of the thunder and rain, which are symbols of Chen and K'an, all between heaven and earth is filled up. But the condition of the time is full of irregularity and obscurity. Feudal princes should be established, but the feeling that rest and peace have been secured should not be indulged even then.

The trigram representing clouds and that representing thunder form Chun. The superior man, in accordance with this, adjusts his measures of government as in sorting the threads of the warp and woof.

1. Although "there is a difficulty in advancing," the mind of the subject of the line is set on doing what is correct. While noble, he humbles himself to the mean and grandly gains the people.

2. The difficulty to the subject of the second line, yin, arises from its place over the yang line below it.

"The union and children after ten years" shows things resuming their regular course.

3. "One pursues the deer without the guidance of the forester": he does so in his eagerness to follow the game. "The superior man gives up the chase, knowing that if he go forward he will regret it": he would be reduced to extremity.

4. "Going forward after such a search for a helper" shows intelligence.

5. "Difficulty is experienced by the subject of the fifth line in bestowing his rich favors": the extent to which they reach will not yet be conspicuous.

6. "He weeps tears of blood in streams": how can the state thus emblemed continue long?

FROM THE NOTES OF JAMES LEGGE:

To move and excite is the quality of Chen; perilousness is the quality of K'an. The power to move is likely to produce great effects; to do this in perilous and difficult circumstances requires firmness and correctness.

K'an represents water, especially in the form of rain. Here its symbol is a cloud. The whole hexagram seems to place us in the atmosphere of a thunderous sky overhung with thick and gloomy clouds, when we feel oppressed and distressed. When the thunder has pealed, and the clouds have discharged their burden of rain, the atmosphere is cleared, and there is a feeling of relief.

The character called Chun is pictorial, and was intended to show us how a plant struggles with difficulty out of the earth, rising gradually above the surface. This difficulty, marking the first stages in the growth of a plant, is used to symbolize the struggles that mark the rise of a state out of a condition of disorder.

KEN, MOUNTAIN
over
K'AN, WATER

4   MENG; YOUTH

THE TEXT:

Meng indicates that in the case which it presupposes there will be progress and success. I do not go and seek the youthful and inexperienced, but he comes and seeks me. When he shows the sincerity that marks the first recourse to divination, I instruct him. If he apply a second and third time, that is troublesome; and I do not instruct the troublesome. There will be advantage in being firm and correct.

1. The first line, yin, has respect to the dispelling of ignorance. It will be advantageous to use punishment for that purpose, and to remove the shackles from the mind. But going on in that way of punishment will give occasion for regret.

2. The second line, yang, shows its subject exercising forbearance with the ignorant, in which there will be good fortune; and admitting even the goodness of women, which will also be fortunate. He may be described also as a son able to sustain the burden of his family.

3. The third line, yin, seems to say that one should not marry a woman whose emblem it might be, for when she sees a man of wealth she will not keep her person from him, and in no wise will advantage come from her.

4. The fourth line, yin, shows its subject as if bound in chains of ignorance. There will be occasion for regret.

5. The fifth line, yin, shows its subject as a simple lad without experience. There will be good fortune.

6. In the topmost line, yang, we see one smiting the ignorant youth. But no advantage will come from doing him an injury. Advantage would come from warding off injury from him.

FROM THE WINGS:

In Meng we have the trigram for a mountain, and below it that of a rugged defile with a stream in it. The conditions of peril and arrest of progress suggested by these give the idea in Meng.

"Meng indicates that there will be progress and success": for there is development at work in it, and its time of action is exactly what is right. "I do not seek the youthful and inexperienced; he seeks me": so does will respond to will. "When he shows the sincerity that marks the first recourse to divination, I instruct him": for possessing the qualities of the yang line and being in the central place, the subject of the second line thus speaks. "A second and third application create annoyance, and I do not instruct so as to create annoyance": annoyance, he means, to the ignorant.

The method of dealing with the young and ignorant is to nourish the correct nature belonging to them; this accomplishes the service of the sage.

The trigram representing a mountain, and beneath it that for a spring issuing forth form Meng. The superior man, in accordance with this, strives to be resolute in his conduct and nourishes his virtue.

1. "It will be advantageous to use punishment": the object being to bring under the influence of correcting law.

2. "A son able to sustain the burden of his family": as appears from the reciprocation between this yang line and the yin fifth line.

3. "A woman such as is here represented should not be taken in marriage": her conduct is not agreeable to what is right.

4. "The regret arising from ignorance bound in chains" is due to the special distance of the subject of this line from the solidity shown in lines 2 and 6.

5. "The good fortune belonging to the simple lad without experience" comes from his docility going on to humility.

6. "Advantage will come from warding off injury": the subject of this line above, and ignorant below, all do and are done to in accordance with their nature.

FROM THE NOTES OF JAMES LEGGE:

As K'an shows us plants struggling from beneath the surface, Meng suggests to us the small and undeveloped appearance which they then present; and hence it came to be the symbol of youthful inexperience and ignorance. The object of the hexagram is to show how such a condition should be dealt with by the parent and ruler, whose authority and duty are represented by the two yang lines, 2 and 6. All between the first and last sentences of the T'uan must be taken as an oracular response received by the party divining on the subject of enlightening the youthful ignorant. This accounts for its being more than usually enigmatical, and for its being partly rhythmical.

According to the scheme of the hexagram, the yang

line in topmost place represents one who uses force in the cause of education. But the force is put forth not on the ignorant, but on those who would keep them ignorant.

In the idea of Meng is the symbol of ignorance and inexperience. In the young and ignorant there is "a correct nature": a moral state made for goodness. The efficient teacher directs his efforts to bring this out. The service done will be worthy of "a sage."

K'AN, WATER
over
CH'IEN, HEAVEN

5 HSU; WAITING

THE TEXT

Hsu intimates that, with the sincerity which is declared in it, there will be brilliant success. With firmness there will be good fortune; and it will be advantageous to cross the great stream.

1. The first line, yang, shows its subject waiting in the distant border. It will be well for him constantly to maintain the purpose shown, in which case there will be no error.

2. The second line, yang, shows its subject waiting on the sand of the mountain stream. He will suffer the small injury of being spoken against, but in the end there will be good fortune.

3. The third line, yang, shows its subject in the mud close by the stream. He thereby invites the approach of injury.

4. The fourth line, yin, shows its subject waiting in the place of blood. But he will get out of the cavern.

5. The fifth line, yang, shows its subject waiting amidst the appliances of a feast. Through his firmness and correctness there will be good fortune.

6. The topmost line, yin, shows its subject entered into the cavern. But there are three guests coming, without being urged, to his help. If he receive them respectfully, there will be good fortune in the end.

FROM THE WINGS:

Hsu denotes waiting. The figure shows peril in front; but notwithstanding the firmness and strength indicated by the lower trigram, its subject does not allow himself to be involved in the dangerous defile: it is right he should not be reduced to extremity.

When it is said that, "with the sincerity declared in Hsu, there will be brilliant success, and with firmness there will be good fortune," this is shown by the position of the fifth line in the place assigned by Heaven, and its being the correct position for it, and in the center. "It will be advantageous to go through the great stream": that is, going forward will be followed by meritorious achievement.

The trigram for clouds ascending, over that for sky, forms Hsu. The superior man, in accordance with this, eats and drinks, feasts and enjoys himself as if there were nothing else to employ him.

1. "He is waiting in the distant border": he makes no movement to encounter rashly the difficulties of the situation. "It will be advantageous for him constantly to maintain the purpose thus shown, in which case there will be no error": he will not fail to pursue that regular course.

2. "He is waiting on the sand": he occupies his position in the center with a generous forbearance. Though "he suffer the small injury of being spoken against," he will bring things to a good issue.

3. "He is waiting in the mud": calamity is close at hand, and as it were in the upper trigram. "He himself invites the approach of injury": if he be reverent and careful, he will not be worsted.

4. "He is waiting in the place of blood": he accommodates himself to the circumstances of the time, and harkens to its requirements.

5. "The appliances of a feast, and the good fortune through being firm and correct," are indicated by the position in the central and correct place.

6. "Guests come unurged to give their help, and if the subject of the line receive them respectfully, there will be good fortune in the end": though the occupant and the place are not suited to each other, there has been no great failure in what has been done.

FROM THE NOTES OF JAMES LEGGE:

Hsu means waiting. Strength confronted by peril might be expected to advance boldly and at once to struggle with it; but it takes the wiser plan of waiting till success be sure. This is the lesson of the hexagram.

"The cloud," it is said, "that has risen to the top of the sky has nothing more to do till it is called on, in the harmony of heaven and earth, to discharge its store of rain." The superior man is supposed to be taught by this symbolism to enjoy his idle time, while he is waiting for approach of danger and occasion for action.

CH'IEN, HEAVEN
over
K'AN, WATER

6 SUNG; STRIFE

THE TEXT:

Sung intimates how, though there is sincerity in
one's contention, he will yet meet with opposition and
obstruction; but if he cherish an apprehensive caution,
there will be good fortune, while, if he must prosecute
the contention to the bitter end, there will be evil. It
will be advantageous to see the great man; it will not
be advantageous to cross the great stream.

1. The first line, yin, shows its subject not perpetua-
ting the matter about which the contention is. He will
suffer the small injury of being spoken against, but the
end will be fortunate.

2. The second line, yang, shows its subject unequal
to the contention. If he retire and keep concealed where
the inhabitants of his city are only three hundred famil-
ies, he will fall into no mistake.

3. The third line, yin, shows its subject keeping in
the old place assigned for his support, and firmly correct. Perilous as the position is, there will be good fortune in the end. Should he perchance engage in the
king's business, he will not claim the merit of achievement.

4. The fourth line, yang, shows its subject unequal
to the contention. He returns to the study of Heaven's

ordinances, changes his wish to contend, and rests in being firm and correct. There will be good fortune.

5. The fifth line, yang, shows its subject contending; and with great good fortune.

6. The topmost line, yang, shows how its subject may have the leathern belt conferred on him by the sovereign, and thrice it shall be taken from him in a morning.

From the Wings:

The upper portion of Sung is the trigram representing strength, and the lower that representing peril. The coming together of strength and peril gives the idea in Sung.

"Sung intimates how, though there is sincerity in one's contention, he will yet meet with opposition and obstruction; but if he cherish an apprehensive caution, there will be good fortune": a yang line has come and got the central place in the lower trigram. "If he must prosecute the contention to the bitter end, there will be evil": contention is not a thing to be carried on to extremity. "It will be advantageous to meet with the great man": what he sets a value on is the due mean, and the correct place. "It will not be advantageous to cross the great stream": one attempting to do so would find himself in an abyss.

The trigram representing heaven and that representing water, moving away from each other, form Sung. The superior man, in accordance with this, in the transaction of affairs takes good counsel about his first steps.

1. "He does not perpetuate the matter about which the contention is": contention should not be prolonged. Although "he may suffer the small injury of being spoken against," his argument is clear.

2. "He is unequal to the contention; he retires and keeps concealed, stealthily withdrawing from it": for him from his lower place to contend with the stronger one above, would be to invite calamity, as if he brought it with his hand to himself.

3. "He confines himself to the support assigned to him of old": thus following those above him, he will have good fortune.

4. "He returns to the study of Heaven's ordinances, changes his wish to contend, and rests in being firm and correct": he does not fail in doing what is right.

5. "He contends; and with great fortune": this is shown by his holding the due mean and being in the correct place.

6. "He receives the robe through his contention": but still he is not deserving of respect.

From the Notes of James Legge:

We have strength in the upper trigram, as if to regulate and control the lower, and peril in that lower as if looking out for an opportunity to assail the upper. Or we have one's self in a state of peril matched against strength from without. All this is supposed to give the idea of contention or strife. But the yang line in the center of K'an is emblematic of sincerity, and gives a character to the whole figure. An individual, so represented, will be very wary, and have good fortune; but strife is bad, and if persevered in even by such a one, the effect will be evil.

K'UN, EARTH
over
K'AN, WATER

7   SHIH; HOSTS

THE TEXT:

Shih indicates how, in the case which it supposes, with firmness and correctness and a leader of age and experience, there will be good fortune and no error.

1. The first line, yin, shows the host going forth according to the rules for such a movement. If these be not good, there will be evil.

2. The second line, yang, shows the leader in the midst of the host. There will be good fortune and no error. The king has thrice conveyed to him the orders of his favor.

3. The third line, yin, shows how the host may, possibly, have many inefficient leaders. There will be evil.

4. The fourth line, yin, shows the host in retreat. There is no error.

5. The fifth line, yin, shows birds in the fields, which it will be advantageous to seize and destroy. In that case there will be no error. If the oldest son leads the host, and younger men idly occupy offices assigned to them, however firm and correct he may be, there will be evil.

6. The topmost line, yin, shows the great ruler delivering his charges, appointing some to be rulers of

states, and others to undertake the headship of clans; but small men should not be employed in such positions.

The name Shih describes the multitude of the host. The "firmness and correctness" which the hexagram indicates refer to moral correctness of aim. When the mover is able to use the multitude with such correctness, he may attain to the royal sway.

There is the symbol of strength in the center of the trigram below, and it is responded to by its proper correlate above. The action gives rise to perils, but is in accordance with the best sentiments of men. Its mover may by such action distress all the country, but the people will follow him; there will be good fortune, and what error should there be?

The trigram representing the earth and in the midst of it that representing water, form Shih. The superior man, in accordance with this, nourishes and educates the people, and collects from among them the multitudes of the hosts.

1. "The host goes forth according to the rules for such a movement": if those rules be not observed, there will be evil.

2. "He is in the midst of the host, and there will be good fortune": he has received the favor of Heaven. "The king has thrice conveyed to him the orders of his favor": the king cherishes the myriad regions in his heart.

3. "The host with the possibility of its having many idle leaders": great will be its want of success.

4. "The host is in retreat; but there is no error": there has been no failure in the regular course.

5. "The oldest son leads the host": its movements are directed by him in accordance with his position in the center. "Younger men idly occupy their positions": the employment of such men is improper.

6. "The great ruler delivers his charges": thereby he rightly apportions merit. "Small men should not be employed": they are sure to throw the states into confusion.

FROM THE NOTES OF JAMES LEGGE:

The conduct of military expeditions is denoted by Shih. The yang line in second place should be interpreted of the general. He is strong and correct, and his enterprises will be successful. He is denominated *ch'ang jen*: "an old, experienced man." The other lines, all yin, suggest the idea of a multitude obedient to his orders.

"Perilousness" is the attribute of K'an, the lower trigram, and "docility," or "accordance with others," that of K'un, the upper. War is like "poison" to a country, injurious, and threatening ruin to it. Yet the people will endure and encounter it in behalf of the sovereign whom they esteem and love.

Line 5: "birds in the fields" are emblematic of plunderers and invaders, whom it will be well to destroy.

Chu Hsi says: "As the water is not outside the earth, so soldiers are not outside the people. Therefore if a ruler be able to nourish the people, he can get the multitudes of his hosts."

(Compare with Legge's sample reading of this hexagram, page 75. C.W.)

K'AN, WATER
over
K'UN, EARTH

8 PI; UNION

THE TEXT:

Pi indicates that under the conditions which it supposes there is good fortune. But let the principal party intended in it reexamine himself, as if by divination, whether his virtue be great, unintermitting, and firm. If it be so, there will be no error. Those who have not rest will then come to him; and with those who are too late in coming it will be ill.

1. The first line, yin, shows its subject seeking by his sincerity to win the attachment of his object. There will be no error. Let the breast be full of sincerity as an earthenware vessel is of its contents, and it will in the end bring other advantages.

2. In the second line, yin, we see the movement toward union and attachment proceeding from the inward mind. With firm correctness there will be good fortune.

3. In the third line, yin, we see its subject seeking for union with such as ought not to be associated with.

4. In the fourth line, yin, we see its subject seeking for union with the one beyond himself. With firm correctness there will be good fortune.

5. The fifth line, yang, affords the most illustrious instance of seeking union and attachment. We see the

king urging his pursuit of the game in three directions only, while the people of his towns do not warn one another to prevent it. There will be good fortune.

6. In the topmost line, yin, we see one seeking union and attachment without having taken the first step to such an end. There will be evil.

FROM THE WINGS:

Pi indicates there is good fortune: the name Pi denotes help; and we see in the figure inferiors docilely following their superior. "Let the principal party re-examine himself as if by divination": this follows from the position of the yang line in the center of the upper trigram. "Those who have not rest will come to him": high and low will respond to its subject. "With those who are too late in coming it will be ill": for them the way of good fortune here indicated has been exhausted.

The trigram of earth and over it the trigram representing water form Pi. The ancient kings, in accordance with this, established the various states and maintained an affectionate relation to their princes.

1. From "the seeking union with its object" there will be other advantages.

2. "The movement toward union and attachment proceeds from the inward mind": the party concerned does not fail in what is proper to himself.

3. "Union is sought with such as ought not to be associated with": will not injury be the result?

4. "Union is sought with one beyond himself": he is following the ruler above him.

5. "The good fortune belonging to the most illustrious instance of seeking union and attachment" appears in the correct and central position, the fifth line, yang.

The king's taking only those animals who present themselves, as it were, obediently, is seen in "his allowing the escape of those in front of him." "That the people do not warn one another to prevent such escape" shows how he, in his high eminence, has made them pursue the due course.

6. "He seeks union and attachment without taking the first step to such an end": there is no possibility of a good issue.

FROM THE NOTES OF JAMES LEGGE:

The ancient kings had their great hunting expeditions in the different seasons, and each season had its peculiar rules. But what is stated here was common to all. When the beating was completed, and the shooting was ready to commence, one side of the enclosure into which the game had been driven was left open and unguarded—proof of the royal benevolence which did not want to make an end of all the game. So well known and understood is this benevolence of the model king in the hexagram, that all his people try to give it effect. Thus the union contemplated is shown to be characterized by mutual confidence and appreciation in virtue and benevolence.

"Water upon the face of the earth": an emblem of close union.

SUN, WIND
over
CH'IEN, HEAVEN

9 HSIAO CH'U; SMALL RESTRAINT

THE TEXT:
Hsiao Ch'u indicates that under its conditions there will be progress and success. We see dense clouds but no rain coming from our borders in the west.

1. The first line, yang, shows its subject returning and pursuing his own course. What mistake should he fall into? There will be good fortune.

2. The second line, yang, shows its subject, by the attraction of the former line, returning to the proper course. There will be good fortune.

3. The third line, yang, suggests the idea of a carriage, the strap beneath which has been removed, or of a husband and wife looking on each other with averted eyes.

4. The fourth line, yin, shows its subject possessed of sincerity. The danger of bloodshed is thereby averted, and his ground for apprehension dismissed. There will be no mistake.

5. The fifth line, yang, shows its subject possessed of sincerity, and drawing others to unite with him. Rich in resources, he employs his neighbors in the same cause with himself.

6. The topmost line, yang, shows how the rain has fallen, and the onward progress is stayed. So must we

value the full accumulation of virtue. But a wife exercising restraint, however firm and correct she may be, is in a position of peril, and like the moon approaching to the full. If the superior man prosecute his measures in such circumstances, there will be evil.

FROM THE WINGS:

In Hsiao Ch'u the yin line occupies its proper position, and the lines above and below respond to it. Hence comes the name of Hsiao Ch'u: Small Restraint.

It presents the symbols of strength and flexibility. Strong lines are in the central places, and the will of their subjects will have free course. Thus it indicates progress and success.

"Dense clouds but no rain" indicate the movement of the strong lines still going forward. The "commencing at our western border" indicates that the beneficial influence has not yet been widely displayed.

The trigram representing the sky, and that representing wind moving above it, form Hsiao Ch'u. The superior man, in accordance with this, adorns the outward manifestation of his virtue.

1. "He returns and pursues his own path": it is right that there should be good fortune.

2. "By the attraction of the subject of the former line he returns to its own course," and is in the central place: neither will he err in what is due from him.

3. "Husband and wife look on each other with averted eyes": the subject of line three is like a husband who cannot maintain correctly his relations with his wife.

4. "He is possessed of sincerity; his ground for apprehension is dismissed": the subjects of the lines above agree in aim with him.

5. "He is possessed of sincerity, and draws others to unite with him": he does not use only his own rich resources.

6. "The rain has fallen and the onward progress is stayed": the power denoted in the figure has accumulated to the full. "If the superior man prosecute his measures, there will be evil": he will find himself obstructed.

FROM THE NOTES OF JAMES LEGGE:

The suitability of the symbolism is made all to turn on the wind. "Wind," says Chu Chen, "is simply the air without solid substance; it can restrain, but not for long." The wind moves in the sky for a time, and then ceases.

The restraint can only be small. The attributes of the two parts of the figure do not indicate anything else. The yang, undivided, line represents vigor and activity. Such a line is in the middle of each trigram. There cannot but be progress and success.

Under Line 6 we have a couplet:

> *Lo! rain, lo! the power is full!*
> *Good man! hold hard. Obstructions rule.*

CH'IEN, HEAVEN
over
TUI, MARSH

10 LU; WALK SOFTLY

THE TEXT:

Lu suggests the idea of one treading on the tail of a tiger which does not bite him. There will be progress and success.

1. The first line, yang, shows its subject treading his accustomed path. If he go forward, there will be no error.

2. The second line, yang, shows its subject treading the path that is level and easy; a quiet and solitary man, to whom, if he be firm and correct, there will be good fortune.

3. The third line, yin, shows a one-eyed man who thinks he can see; a lame man who thinks he can walk well; one who treads on the tail of a tiger and is bitten. All this indicates ill fortune. We have a mere bravo acting the part of a great ruler.

4. The fourth line, yang, shows its subject treading on the tail of a tiger. He becomes full of apprehensive caution, and in the end there will be good fortune.

5. The fifth line, yang, shows the resolute tread of its subject. Though he be firm and correct, there will be peril.

6. The sixth line, yang, tells us to look at the whole course that is trodden, and examine the presage which

that gives. If it be complete and without failure, there will be great good fortune.

FROM THE WINGS:

In Lu we have the symbol of weakness treading on that of strength.

The lower trigram indicates pleasure and satisfaction, and responds to the upper indicating strength. Hence it is said, "He treads on the tail of a tiger, which does not bite him; there will be progress and success."

The fifth line is yang in the center and in its correct place. Its subject occupies the God-given position, and falls into no distress or failure; his action will be brilliant.

The trigram representing the sky above, and below it that representing the waters of a marsh, form Lu. The superior man, in accordance with this, discriminates between high and low, and gives settlement to the aims of the people.

1. "He treads his accustomed path and goes forward": singly and exclusively he carries out his long-cherished wishes.

2. "A quiet and solitary man, to whom, being firm and correct, there will be good fortune": holding the due mean, he will not allow himself to be thrown into disorder.

3. "A one-eyed man who thinks that he can see": he is not fit to see clearly. "A lame man who thinks that he can tread well": one cannot walk along with him. "The ill fortune of being bitten" arises from the place not being the proper one for him. "A mere bravo acting the part of a great ruler": this is owing to his aims being too violent.

4. "He becomes full of apprehensive caution, and effect.

5. "He treads resolutely; and though he be firm and correct, there is peril": this is due to his being in the position that is correct and appropriate to him.

6. "There will be great good fortune," and that in the occupancy of the topmost line: this is great matter for congratulation.

FROM THE NOTES OF JAMES LEGGE:

"Treading on a tiger's tail" is an old way of expressing what was hazardous. The attribute of Tui, Marsh, is pleased satisfaction; this suggests the statement that "the tiger does not bite the treader."

"The sky above and a marsh lying below it is true," says Cheng K'ang Ch'eng, "in nature and reason; and so should be the rules of propriety on which men tread." This symbolism is farfetched; but it is true that the members of a community must keep their several places and duties to preserve order. The principle underlying Line 5 is that the most excellent thing in "propriety" is humility. The subject of the line will not be lacking in this, but bear in mind that the higher he is exalted, the greater may be his fall.

K'UN, EARTH
over
CH'IEN, HEAVEN

11   T'AI; THE WAXING

THE TEXT:

In T'ai we see the little gone and the great come. It indicates that there will be good fortune, with progress and success.

1. The first line, yang, suggests the idea of grass pulled up, and bringing with it other stalks with whose roots it is connected. Advance on the part of its subject will be fortunate.

2. The second line, yang, shows one who can bear with the uncultivated, will cross the Ho without a boat, does not forget the distant, and has no selfish friendships. Thus does he prove himself acting in accordance with the course of the due mean.

3. The third line, yang, shows that, while there is no state of peace that is not liable to be disturbed, and no departure of evil men so that they shall not return, yet when one is firm and correct, as he realizes the distresses that may arise he will commit no error. There is no occasion for sadness at the certainty of such recurring changes; and in this mood the happiness of the present may be long enjoyed.

4. The fourth line, yin, shows its subject fluttering down; not relying on his own rich resources, but calling in his neighbors. They all come not as having received warning, but in the sincerity of their hearts.

5. The fifth line, yin, reminds us of king Ti-yi's rule about the marriage of his younger sister. By such a course there is happiness and there will be great good fortune.

6. The sixth line, yin, shows us the city wall returned into the moat. It is not the time to use the army. The subject of the line may, indeed, announce his orders to the people of his own city; but however correct and firm he may be he will have cause for regret.

FROM THE WINGS:

"The little gone and the great come in T'ai, and its indication that there will be good fortune with progress and success" show to us heaven and earth in communication with each other, and all things in consequence having free course, and also the high and the low, superiors and inferiors, in communication with one another, and possessed by the same aim. The inner trigram is made up of the yang lines and the outer of the yin; the inner is the symbol of strength, and the outer of docility; the inner represents the superior man, and the outer the small man. Thus the way of the superior man appears increasing, and that of the small man decreasing.

The trigrams for heaven and earth in communication together form T'ai. The sage, in harmony with this, fashions and completes his regulations after the courses of heaven and earth, and assists the application of the adaptations furnished by them in order to benefit the people.

1. "The good fortune of advance, as suggested by the emblem of the grass pulled up," arises from the will of

the party intended being set on what is external to himself.

2. "He bears with the uncultivated, and proves himself acting in accordance with the due mean": for his intelligence is bright and his capacity is great.

3. "There is no going away so that there shall not be a return" refers to this as the point where the interaction of heaven and earth takes place.

4. "He comes fluttering down, not relying on his own rich resources": both he and his neighbors are out of their real place. "They have not received warning, but come in the sincerity of their hearts": this is what they have desired in the core of their hearts.

5. "By such a course there is happiness, and there will be great good fortune": the subject of the line employs the virtue proper to his central position to carry his wishes into effect.

6. "The city wall returned back into the moat" shows how the governmental orders have long been in disorder.

FROM THE NOTES OF JAMES LEGGE:

The "gone" and "come" are equivalent to "below" and "above"; lower trigram, upper trigram.

A course in which the motive forces are represented by the three yang lines, and the opposing by the three yin, must be progressive and successful.

T'ai is called the hexagram of the first month of the year, the first month of the natural spring, when for six months under genial skies and the fostering sun processes of growth will be going on.

CH'IEN, HEAVEN
over
K'UN, EARTH

12 P'I; THE WANING

THE TEXT:

In P'i there is the want of good understanding between the different classes of men, and its indication is unfavorable to the firm and correct course of the superior man. We see in it the great gone and the little come.

1. The first line, yin, suggests the idea of grass pulled up, and bringing with it other stalks with whose roots it is connected. With firm correctness on the part of its subject, there will be good fortune and progress.

2. The second line, yin, shows its subject patient and obedient. To the small man comporting himself so, there will be good fortune. If the great man comport himself as the distress and obstruction require, he will have success.

3. The third line, yin, shows its subject ashamed of the purpose folded in his breast.

4. The fourth line, yang, shows its subject acting in accordance with the ordination of Heaven, and committing no error. His companions will come and share in his happiness.

5. In the fifth line, yang, we see him who brings the distress and obstruction to a close, the great man and fortunate. But let him say, "We may perish! We may

perish!" So shall the state of things stagnate as if bound to a clump of bushy mulberry trees.

6. The sixth line, yang, shows the overthrow and removal of the condition of distress and obstruction. Before this there was that condition. Hereafter there will be joy.

FROM THE WINGS:

"The want of good understanding between the different classes of men in P'i, and its indication as unfavorable to the firm and correct course of the superior man; with the intimation that the great are gone and the little come": all this springs from the fact that in it heaven and earth are not in communication with each other, and all things in consequence do not have free course; and that the high and the low, superiors and inferiors, are not in communication with one another, and there are no well-regulated states under the sky. The inner trigram is made up of yin lines, and the outer of the yang; the inner is the symbol of weakness, and the outer of strength; the inner represents the small man, and the outer the superior man. Thus the way of the small man appears increasing, and that of the superior man decreasing.

The trigrams of heaven and earth, not in intercommunication, form P'i. The superior man, in accordance with this, restrains the manifestation of his virtue, and avoids the calamities that threaten him. There is no opportunity of conferring on him the glory of office.

1. "The good fortune through firm goodness, suggested by the pulling up of grass," arises from the will of the parties intended being bent on serving the ruler.

2. "The great man, comporting himself as the distress

and obstruction require, will have success": he does not allow himself to be disordered by the herd of small men.

3. That "his shame is folded in his breast" is owing to the inappropriateness of his position.

4. "He acts in accordance with the ordination of Heaven, and commits no error": the purpose of his mind can be carried into effect.

5. "The good fortune of the great man" arises from the correctness of his position.

6. "The distress and obstruction having reached its end, it is overthrown and removed": how could it be prolonged?

FROM THE NOTES OF JAMES LEGGE:

The form of P'i is exactly the opposite of T'ai. Much of what has been said there will apply here. P'i is the hexagram of the seventh month. Genial influences have done their work; the processes of growth are at an end. Henceforth decay must be looked for.

The yang line in the fifth and correct place brings distress and obstruction to a close. Yet its subject is warned to continue to be cautious in two lines of rhyme:

And let him say, "I die! I die!"
So to a bushy clump his fortune he shall tie.

CH'IEN, HEAVEN
over
LI, FIRE

13   T'UNG JEN; BROTHERHOOD

THE TEXT:

T'ung Jen or "Union of men" appears here as we find it in the remote districts of the country, indicating progress and success. It will be advantageous to cross the great stream. It will be advantageous to maintain the firm correctness of the superior man.

1. The first line, yang, shows the representative of the union of men just issuing from his gate. There will be no error.

2. The second line, yin, shows the representative of the union of men in relation with his kindred. There will be occasion for regret.

3. The third line, yang, shows its subject with his arms hidden in the thick grass, and at the top of a high mound. But for three years he makes no demonstration.

4. The fourth line, yang, shows its subject mounted on the city wall; but he does not proceed to make the attack he contemplates. There will be good fortune.

5. In the fifth line, yang, the representative of the union of men first wails and cries out, and then laughs. His great host conquers, and he and the subject of the second line meet together.

6. The topmost line, yang, shows the representative of the union of men in the suburbs. There will be no occasion for repentance.

FROM THE WINGS:

In T'ung Jen the yin line has the place of influence, the central place, and responds to the corresponding line in Ch'ien above; hence comes its name "Union of men."

The language, "T'ung Jen appears here as we find it in the remote districts of the country, indicating progress and success, and that it will be advantageous to cross the great stream," is molded by its containing the strength symboled in Ch'ien. Then we have the trigram indicating elegance and intelligence, supported by that indicating strength; with the line in the central, and its correct, position, and responding to the corresponding line above: all representing the correct course of the superior man. It is only the superior man who can comprehend and affect the minds of all under the sky.

The trigrams for heaven and fire form T'ung Jen. The superior man, in accordance with this, distinguishes things according to their kinds and classes.

1. "The representative of the union of men is just issuing from his gate": who will blame him?

2. "The representative of the union of men appears in relation with his kindred": that is the path to regret.

3. "He hides his arms in the thick grass": because of the strength of his opponent. "For three years he makes no demonstration": how can he do anything?

4. "He is mounted on his city-wall"; but yielding to the right, "he does not proceed to make the attack he contemplated." Where it is said, "There will be good fortune," that shows how he feels the strait he is in, and returns to the rule of law.

5. The first action of the representative of the union

of men here described arises from his central position and straightforward character. "The meeting secured by his great host" intimates that the opponents of it have been overcome.

6. "The representative of the union of men appears in the suburbs": his object has not yet been attained.

FROM THE NOTES OF JAMES LEGGE:

T'ung Jen describes a condition of nature and of the state opposed to that of P'i. There was distress and obstruction; here is union.

The union must be free from all selfish motives, and this is indicated by its being in the remote districts of the country, where people are unsophisticated, and free from the depraving effects incident to large societies.

The style of "heaven and fire form T'ung Jen" is such as to suggest the appearance of fire ascending, blazing to the sky, and uniting with it.

LI, FIRE
over
CH'IEN, HEAVEN

14   Ta Yu; Great Havings

The Text:

Ta Yu indicates that, under the circumstances which it implies, there will be great progress and success.

1. In the first line, yang, there is no approach to what is injurious, and there is no error. Let there be a realization of the difficulty and danger of the position, and there will be no error to the end.

2. In the second line, yang, we have a large wagon with its load. In whatever direction advance is made, there will be no error.

3. The third line, yang, shows us a feudal prince presenting his offerings to the Son of Heaven. A small man would be unequal to such a duty.

4. The fourth line, yang, shows its subject keeping his great resources under restraint. There will be no error.

5. The fifth line, yin, shows the sincerity of its subject reciprocated by that of all the others represented in the hexagram. Let him display a proper majesty, and there will be good fortune.

6. The topmost line, yang, shows its subject with help accorded to him from Heaven. There will be good fortune, advantage in every respect.

FROM THE WINGS:

In Ta Yu the yin line has the place of honor, is grandly central, and the strong lines above and below respond to it. Hence comes its name of Ta Yu, Having what is Great.

The attributes of its component trigrams are strength and vigor with elegance and brightness. The ruling line in it responds to the ruling line in the symbol of heaven, and consequently its action is all at the proper time. In this way it is said to indicate great progress and success.

The trigram for heaven and that of fire above it form Ta Yu. The superior man, in accordance with this, represses what is evil and gives distinction to what is good, in sympathy with the excellent Heaven-conferred nature.

1. This first line, yang, of Ta Yu shows no approach to what is injurious.

2. "A large wagon with its load" refers to the virtue accumulated in the subject of the line, so that he will suffer no loss in the conduct of affairs.

3. "A feudal prince presents his offerings to the Son of Heaven": a small man in such a position does himself harm.

4. "He keeps his great resources under restraint": his wisdom discriminates clearly what he ought to do.

5. "His sincerity is reciprocated by all the others": his sincerity serves to stir and call out what is in their minds. "The good fortune springing from a display of proper majesty" shows how they might otherwise feel too easy, and make no preparation to serve him.

6. The good fortune attached to the topmost line of Ta Yu arises from the help of Heaven.

FROM THE NOTES OF JAMES LEGGE:

The danger threatening a condition of opulence is the pride which it is likely to engender. But everything here is against that issue: we have the place of honor occupied by a yin line, so that its subject will be humble. All the other lines, strong as they are, will act in obedient sympathy. There will be great progress and success.

"Fire above the sky" will shine far; this symbolizes the vastness of the territory, or of the wealth implied, in the possession of what is great.

K'UN, EARTH
over
KEN, MOUNTAIN

15 Ch'ien; Humility

The Text:

Ch'ien indicates progress and success. The superior man, being humble as it implies, will have a good issue to his undertakings.

1. The first line, yin, shows us the superior man who adds humility to humility. Even the great stream may be crossed with this, and there will be good fortune.

2. The second line, yin, shows us humility that has made itself recognized. With firm correctness there will be good fortune.

3. The third line, yang, shows the superior man of acknowledged merit. He will maintain his success to the end, and have good fortune.

4. The fourth line, yin, shows one, whose action would be in every way advantageous, stirring up the more his humility.

5. The fifth line, yin, shows one who, without being rich, is able to employ his neighbors. He may advantageously use the force of arms. All his movements will be advantageous.

6. The sixth line, yin, shows us humility that has made itself recognized. The subject of it will with advantage put his hosts in motion; but he will only punish his own towns and state.

FROM THE WINGS:

Ch'ien indicates progress and success. It is the way of heaven to send down its beneficial influences, where they are brilliantly displayed. It is the way of earth, lying low, to send its influences upward and there to act.

It is the way of heaven to diminish the full and augment the humble. It is the way of earth to overthrow the full and replenish the humble. Spiritual Beings inflict calamity on the full and bless the humble. It is the way of men to hate the full and love the humble. Humility in a position of honor makes that still more brilliant; and in a low position men will not seek to pass beyond it. Thus it is that "the superior man will have a good issue to his undertakings."

The trigram for the earth and that of a mountain in the midst of it form Ch'ien. The superior man, in accordance with this, diminishes what is excessive in himself, and increases where there is defect, bringing about an equality, according to the nature of the case, in his treatment of himself and others.

1. "The superior man who adds humility to humility" is one who nourishes his virtue in lowliness.

2. "The good fortune consequent on being firm and correct, where the humility has made itself recognized," is owing to the possessor's having the virtue in the core of his heart.

3. "The superior man of acknowledged merit, and yet humble": the myriads of the people will submit to him.

4. "One, whose action would be in every way advantageous, stirs up his humility the more": but in doing so he does not act contrary to the proper rule.

5. "He may advantageously use the force of arms": correcting, that is, those who do not submit.

6. "His humility has made itself recognized": but all his aims have not yet been attained. "He may employ the force of arms, but only in correcting his own towns and state."

FROM THE NOTES OF JAMES LEGGE:

An essay on humility rightly follows that on abundant possessions. Humility is the way to permanent success. The descent of the heavenly influences, and the low position of the earth are both emblematic of humility.

"Spiritual Beings" are represented by k'uei-shen. The term k'uei denotes specially the human spirit disembodied, and shen is used for spirits whose seat is in heaven. I do not see my way to translate them, when used together, otherwise than by spiritual beings or spiritual agents.

CHEN, THUNDER
over
K'UN, EARTH

16 YU; HARMONY

THE TEXT:

Yu indicates that, in the state which it implies, feudal princes may be set up, and the hosts put in motion, with advantage.

1. The first line, yin, shows its subject proclaiming his pleasure and satisfaction. There will be evil.

2. The second line, yin, shows one who is firm as a rock. He sees a thing without waiting till it has come to pass; with his firm correctness there will be good fortune.

3. The third line, yin, shows one looking up for favors, while he indulges the feeling of pleasure and satisfaction. If he would understand! If he be late in doing so, there will indeed be occasion for repentance.

4. The fourth line, yang, shows him from whom the harmony and satisfaction come. Great is the success which he obtains. Let him not allow suspicions to enter his mind, and thus friends will gather around him.

5. The fifth line, yin, shows one with a chronic complaint, but who lives on without dying.

6. The topmost line, yin, shows its subject with darkened mind devoted to the pleasure and satisfaction of the time; but if he change his course even when it may be considered as completed, there will be no error.

FROM THE WINGS:

In Yu we see the yang line responded to by all the others, and the will of him whom it represents being carried out; and also docile obedience employing movement for its purposes. From these things comes Yu, the condition of harmony and satisfaction.

In this condition we have docile obedience employing movement for its purposes, and therefore it is so as between heaven and earth; how much more will it be so among men in "the setting up of feudal princes and putting the hosts in motion"!

Heaven and earth show that docile obedience in connection with movement, and hence the sun and moon make no error in time, and the four seasons do not deviate from their order. The sages show such docile obedience in connection with their movements, and hence their punishments and penalties are entirely just, and the people acknowledge it by their submission. Great indeed are the time and significance indicated in Yu!

The trigrams for the Earth and Thunder issuing from it with its crashing noise form Yu. The ancient kings, in accordance with this, composed their music and did honor to virtue, presenting it especially and most grandly to God, when they associated with Him to serve their highest ancestor and their father.

1. "The subject of the first line proclaims his pleasure and satisfaction": there will be evil; his wishes have been satisfied to overflowing.

2. "He sees a thing without waiting till it has come to pass; with his firm correctness there will be good fortune": this is shown by the central and correct position of the line.

3. "He looks up for favors, while he indulges the feeling of satisfaction; there will be occasion for repentance": this is intimated by the position not being the appropriate one.

4. "From him the harmony and satisfaction come; great is the success which he obtains": his aims take effect on a grand scale.

5. "The subject of the fifth line has a chronic complaint": this is shown by his being mounted on the strong line. "He still lives on without dying": he is in the central position, and its memories of the past have not yet perished.

6. "With darkened mind devoted to the harmony and satisfaction of the time," as shown in the topmost line: how can one in such a condition continue long?

FROM THE NOTES OF JAMES LEGGE:

Yu: Condition of harmony; happy contentment.

"Obedience" is the attribute of K'un, the lower trigram which takes the initiative in the action of the figure, and here makes use of *movement*, the attribute of Chen, the upper trigram.

The use of music at sacrifices to assist the union produced by those services between God and his worshipers and the present and past generations, agree with the general idea of this figure.

TUI, MARSH
over
CHEN, THUNDER

17   SUI; FOLLOWING

THE TEXT:

Sui indicates that under its conditions there will be great progress and success. But it will be advantageous to be firm and correct. There will then be no error.

1. The first line, yang, shows us one changing the object of his pursuit; but if he be firm and correct, there will be good fortune. Going beyond his own gate to find associates, he will achieve merit.

2. The second line, yin, shows us one who cleaves to the little boy, and lets go the man of age and experience.

3. The third line, yin, shows us one who cleaves to the man of age and experience, and lets go the little boy. Such following will get what it seeks; but it will be advantageous to adhere to what is firm and correct.

4. The fourth line, yang, shows us one followed and obtaining adherents. Though he be firm and correct, there will be evil. If he be sincere, however, in his course, and make that evident, into what error will he fall?

5. The fifth line, yang, shows us the ruler sincere in fostering all that is excellent. There will be good fortune.

6. The topmost line, yin, shows us that sincerity firmly

held and clung to and bound fast. We see the king with it presenting his offerings on the western mountain.

In Sui we see the attributes of movement and pleasure: this gives the idea of Sui.

"There will be great progress and success; and through firm correctness no error": all under heaven will be found following at such a time.

Great indeed are the time and significance indicated in Sui.

The trigram for the waters of a marsh and that for thunder hidden in the midst of it form Sui. The superior man in accordance with this, when it is getting toward dark, enters his house and rests.

1. "He is changing the object of his pursuit": but if he follow what is correct, there will be good fortune. "He goes beyond his own gate to find associates": he will not fail in the method he pursues.

2. "He cleaves to the little boy": he cannot be with the two at the same time.

3. "He cleaves to the man of age and experience": by the decision of his will, he abandons the youth below.

4. "He is followed and obtains adherents": according to the idea of the hexagram, this is evil. "He is sincere in his course": showing his intelligence, and leading to achievement.

5. "He is sincere in fostering what is excellent": his position is correct and in the center.

6. "The sincerity is firmly held and clung to, as shown

in the topmost line": the idea of the hexagram has reached its extreme development.

FROM THE NOTES OF JAMES LEGGE:

Sui symbolizes the idea of following, directed by the most sincere adherence to what is right. The hexagram includes the cases where one follows others, and where others follow him. The auspice of great progress and success is due to this flexibility and applicability of it.

An explosion of thunder amidst the waters of a marsh would be succeeded by a tremulous agitation of those waters. In the application of the symbolism we have an illustration of action according to, or following, the time, which is a common use of the Chinese character Sui.

"The western hill" is mount Ch'i, at the foot of which was the original settlement of the house of Chou, in B.C. 1325.

KEN, MOUNTAIN
over
SUN, WIND

18   Ku; Work To Be Done

THE TEXT:

Ku indicates great progress and success to him who deals properly with the condition represented by it. There will be advantage in efforts like that of crossing the great stream. He should weigh well, however, the events of three days before the turning point, and those to be done three days after it.

1. The first line, yin, shows a son dealing with the troubles caused by his father. If he be an able son, the father will escape the blame of having erred. The position is perilous, but there will be good fortune in the end.

2. The second line, yang, shows a son dealing with the troubles caused by his mother. He should not carry his firm correctness to the utmost.

3. The third line, yang, shows a son dealing with the troubles caused by his father. There may be some small occasion for repentance, but there will not be any great error.

4. The fourth line, yin, shows a son viewing indulgently the troubles caused by his father. If he go forward, he will find cause to regret it.

5. The fifth line, yin, shows a son dealing with the troubles caused by his father. He obtains the praise of using the fit instrument for his work.

6. The sixth line, yang, shows us one who does not serve either king or feudal lord, but in a lofty spirit prefers to attend to his own affairs.

FROM THE WINGS:

In Ku we have a strong trigram above and a weak one below; we have below pliancy, and above stopping; these give the idea of a Troublous Condition of affairs verging to ruin.

"Ku indicates great progress and success": through the course shown in it, all under heaven, there will be good order. "There will be advantage in crossing the great stream": he who advances will encounter the business to be done. "He should weigh well, however, the events of three days before the turning-point, and those to be done three days after it": the end of confusion is the beginning of order; such is the procedure of Heaven.

The trigram for a mountain, and below it that for wind, form Ku. The superior man, in accordance with this, addresses himself to help the people and nourish his own virtue.

1. "He deals with the troubles caused by his father": he feels that he has entered into the work of his father.

2. "He deals with the troubles caused by his mother'": he holds to the course of the due mean.

3. "He deals with the troubles caused by his father": in the end there will be no error.

4. "He views indulgently the troubles caused by his father": if he go forward, he will not succeed.

5. "He deals with the troubles caused by his father, and obtains praise": he is responded to by the subject of line 2 with all his virtue.

6. "He does not serve either king or feudal lord": but his aim may be a model to others.

FROM THE NOTES OF JAMES LEGGE:
Feeble pliancy confronted by the arresting mountain gives an idea of the evil state implied in Ku. Ku means the having painful or troublesome services to do. It denotes here a state in which things are going to ruin as if through poison or venomous worms; and the figure is supposed to describe the arrest of the decay and the restoration to soundness and vigor, so as to justify its auspice of great progress and success. To realize such a result, however, great efforts will be required, as in crossing the great stream.

By giving heed to the cautions in the text, the subject will accomplish what is promised. This is "course of the due mean."

"Three days before and after the turning-point" is, literally, "three days before and after chia," chia being the name of the first of the "earthly stems" among the cyclical characters. Hence it has the meaning of "beginning," and here denotes the turning-point, at which disorder gives place to order. According to "the procedure of Heaven," history is a narrative of change, one condition of affairs constantly giving place to another and opposite. "A kingdom that cannot be moved" does not enter into the circle of Chinese ideas.

"When the wind," says Cheng K'ang Ch'eng, "encounters the mountain, it is driven back, and the things about are all scattered in disorder; such is the emblem of the state denoted by Ku."

K'UN, EARTH
over
TUI, MARSH

19 Lin; Authority Comes

The Text:

Lin indicates that under the conditions supposed in it there will be great progress and success, while it will be advantageous to be firmly correct. In the eighth month there will be evil.

1. The first line, yang, shows its subject advancing in company with the subject of the second line. Through his firm correctness there will be good fortune.

2. The second line, yang, shows its subject advancing in company with the subject of the first line. There will be good fortune; advancing will be in every way advantageous.

3. The third line, yin, shows one well pleased indeed to advance, but whose action will be in no way advantageous. If he become anxious about it, however, there will be no error.

4. The fourth line, yin, shows one advancing in the highest mode. There will be no error.

5. The fifth line, yin, shows the advance of wisdom, such as befits the great ruler. There will be good fortune.

6. The sixth line, yin, shows the advance of honesty and generosity. There will be good fortune and no error.

In Lin we see the yang lines gradually increasing and advancing.

The lower trigram is the symbol of being pleased, and the upper of being compliant. The yang line is in the central position and is properly responded to.

"There is great progress and success, along with firm correctness": this is the way of Heaven.

"In the eighth month there will be evil": the advancing power will decay after no long time.

The trigram for the waters of a marsh and that for the earth above it form Lin. The superior man, in accordance with this, has his purposes of instruction that are inexhaustible, and nourishes and supports the people without limit.

1. "The good fortune through the firm correctness of the subject of the first line advancing in company with the subject of the second" is due to his will being set on doing what is right.

2. "The good fortune and every possible advantage attending the advance of the subject of the second line, in company with the subject of the first," arises from the fact that those to whom the advance is made are not yet obedient to the ordinances of Heaven.

3. "He shows himself well pleased to advance": his position is not that appropriate to him. "If he become anxious, however, about his action," his error will not be continued.

4. "The freedom from error consequent on the advance in the highest mode" is due to the various appropriateness of the position.

5. "What befits the great ruler" means the pursuing the course of the due mean.

6. "The good fortune consequent on the advance of honesty and generosity" is due to the will of the subject of the line being set on the subjects of the first two lines of the inner trigram.

FROM THE NOTES OF JAMES LEGGE:

Lin denotes the approach of authority, to inspect, to comfort, or to rule.

20 KUAN; MANIFESTING AND CONTEMPLATING

THE TEXT:
Kuan shows how he whom it represents should be like the worshiper who has washed his hands, but not yet presented his offerings; with sincerity and an appearance of dignity commanding reverent regard.

1. The first line, yin, shows the looking of a lad; not blamable in men of inferior rank, but matter for regret in superior men.

2. The second line, yin, shows one peeping out from a door. It would be advantageous if it were merely the firm correctness of a female.

3. The third line, yin, shows one looking at the course of his own life, to advance to recede accordingly.

4. The fourth line, yin, shows one contemplating the glory of the kingdom. It will be advantageous for him, being such as he is, to seek to be a guest of the king.

5. The fifth line, yang, shows its subject contemplating his own life-course. A superior man, he will thus fall into no error.

6. The sixth line, yang, shows its subject contemplating his character to see if it be indeed that of a superior man. He will not fall in error.

FROM THE WINGS:
The great Manifester occupies an upper place in the

figure, which consists of the trigrams whose attributes are docility and flexibility. He is in the central position and his correct place, and thus exhibits his lessons to all under heaven.

"Kuan shows its subject like a worshiper who has washed his hands, but not yet presented his offerings; with sincerity and an appearance of dignity commanding reverent regard": all beneath look to him and are transformed.

When we contemplate the spirit-like way of Heaven, we see how the four seasons proceed without error. The sages, in accordance with this spirit-like way, laid down their instructions, and all under heaven yield submission to them.

The trigram representing the earth, and that for wind moving above it, form Kuan. The ancient kings, in accordance with this, examined the different regions of the kingdom, to see the ways of the people, and set forth their instructions.

1. "The looking of a lad shown by the first line, yin," indicates the way of the inferior people.

2. "The firm correctness of a woman, in peeping out from a door" is also a thing to be ashamed of in a superior man.

3. "He looks at the course of his own life, to advance or recede accordingly": he will not err in the path to be pursued.

4. "He contemplates the glory of the kingdom": thence arises the wish to be a guest at court.

5. "He contemplates his own life-course": he should for this purpose contemplate the condition of the people.

6. "He contemplates his own character": he cannot even yet let his mind be at rest.

FROM THE NOTES OF JAMES LEGGE:

The Chinese character Kuan, from which this hexagram is named, is used in it in two senses. It denotes showing, manifesting, and also contemplating, looking at. The subject of the hexagram is the sovereign and his subjects, how he manifests himself to them, and how they contemplate him. The two upper, yang, lines belong to the sovereign; the four yin lines below them are his subjects—ministers and others who look up at him.

"The great Manifester" is the ruler. The lower trigram is K'un, representing the earth, with the attribute of docility, and the upper is Sun, representing wind, with the attributes of flexibility and penetration.

"The spirit-like way of Heaven" is the invisible and unfathomable agency ever operating by general laws, and with invariable regularity, in what we call nature.

Wind moving above the earth has the widest sweep, and nothing escapes its influence; it penetrates everywhere. This symbolism is more appropriate to the subject in hand than that of many other hexagrams. Personal influence in a ruler effects much; but the ancient kings wished to add to that the power of published instructions, specially adapted to the character and circumstances of the people. Sun, representing the wind, is well adapted to denote this influence.

LI, FIRE
over
CHEN, THUNDER

21   SHIH HO; UNION BY GNAWING

THE TEXT:

Shih Ho indicates successful progress in the condition of things which it supposes. It will be advantageous to use legal constraints.

1. The first line, yang, shows one with his feet in the stocks and deprived of his toes. There will be no error.

2. The second line, yin, shows one biting through the soft flesh, and going on to bite off the nose. There will be no error.

3. The third line, yin, shows one gnawing dried flesh, and meeting with what is disagreeable. There will be occasion for some small regret, but no great error.

4. The fourth line, yang, shows one gnawing the flesh dried on the bone, and getting the pledges of money and arrows. It will be advantageous to him to realize the difficulty of his task and be firm, in which case there will be good fortune.

5. The fifth line, yin, shows one gnawing at dried flesh, and finding the yellow gold. Let him be firm and correct, realizing the peril of his position. There will be no error.

6. The sixth line, yang, shows one wearing the cangue, and deprived of his ears. There will be evil.

FROM THE WINGS:

The existence of something between the jaws gives rise to the name of Shih Ho, Union by means of biting through the intervening article. This indicates the "successful progress" denoted by the hexagram.

The yang and yin lines are equally divided. Movement is denoted by the lower trigram, and bright intelligence by the upper; thunder and lightning uniting, and having brilliant manifestation. The fifth line, yin, is in the center, and acts in its high position; although not in its proper position, this is advantageous for the use of legal constraints.

The trigrams representing thunder and lightning form Shih Ho. The ancient kings, in accordance with this, framed their penalties with intelligence, and promulgated their laws.

1. "His feet are in the stocks, and he is deprived of his toes": there is no walking to do evil.

2. "He bites through the soft flesh, and goes on to bite off the nose": the subject of the line is mounted on the strong first line.

3. "He meets with what is disagreeable and hurtful": his position is not the proper one for him.

4. "It will be advantageous to him to realize the difficulty of his task and be firm, in which case there will be good fortune": his light has not yet been sufficiently displayed.

5. "Let him be firm and correct, realizing the peril of his position, and there will be no error": he will possess every quality appropriate to his position and task.

6. "He wears the cangue and is deprived of his ears": he hears, but will not understand.

From the Notes of James Legge:

"Union by gnawing" suggests the idea of the mouth kept open by something in it. Let that be gnawed through and the mouth will close and the jaws come together. So in the body politic. Remove the obstacles to union, and high and low will come together with a good understanding. How are those obstacles to be removed? By force, emblemed by the gnawing: that is, by legal constraint. And these are sure to be successful. The auspice of the figure is favorable. There will be success.

The punishment in Line 1 is that of the stocks: administered for a small offense, before crime has made much way.

The action of the subject of Line 2 should be effective: "biting through the soft flesh" is an easy thing.

Line 3 shows the action of its subject will be ineffective, emblemed by the hard task of gnawing through dried flesh, and encountering besides what is distasteful and injurious. But again comes in the consideration that here punishment is the rule, and the auspice is not all bad.

Of old, in a civil case, both parties, before they were heard, brought to the court an arrow or bundle of arrows, in testimony of their rectitude, after which they were heard. In a criminal case, they deposited thirty pounds of gold, or some other metal. The subject of Line 4, getting those pledges, indicates his exercising his judicial functions; what he gnaws through indicates their difficulty. Hence the lesson of caution.

Line 5 represents a judgment of leniency. This is declared by "yellow" metal.

In Line 6 we have the subject, persisting in wrong, wearing the square collar (cangue) used to confine criminals, and deaf to counsel. Of course the auspice is evil.

Cheng K'ang Ch'eng says that thunder and lightning are always found together, and their trigrams give the idea of the union intended by Shih Ho.

KEN, MOUNTAIN
over
LI, FIRE

22   Pɪ; Adornment

THE TEXT:

Pi indicates that there should be free course in what it denotes. There will be little advantage, however, if it be allowed to advance and take the lead.

1. The first line, yang, shows one adorning the way of his feet. He can discard a carriage and walk on foot.

2. The second line, yin, shows one adorning his beard.

3. The third line, yang, shows its subject with the appearance of being adorned with rich favors. But let him ever maintain his firm correctness, and there will be good fortune.

4. The fourth line, yin, shows one looking as if adorned, but only in white. As if mounted on a white horse, and furnished with wings, he seeks union with the subject of the first line, while the intervening third pursues, not as a robber, but intent on a matrimonial alliance.

5. The fifth line, yin, shows its subject adorned by the occupants of the heights and gardens. He bears his roll of silk, small and slight. He may appear stingy; but there will be good fortune in the end.

6. The sixth line, yang, shows one with white as his only ornament. There will be no error.

FROM THE WINGS:

Elegance and intelligence, denoted by the lower trigram, Li, regulated by the arrest denoted by the upper, Ken, suggest the observances that adorn human society.

We look at the ornamental figures of the sky, and thereby ascertain the changes of the seasons. We look at the ornamental observance of society, and understand how the processes of transformation are accomplished all under heaven.

The trigram representing Mountain and that for Fire under it form Pi. The superior man, in accordance with this, throws a brilliancy around his various processes of government, but does not decide cases of criminal litigation.

1. "He can discard a carriage and walk on foot": righteousness requires that he should not ride.

2. "He adorns his beard": he rouses himself to action only along with the subject of the line above.

3. "The good fortune consequent on his ever maintaining firm correctness" is due to this, that to the end no one will insult him.

4. "The place occupied by the fourth line, yin," affords ground for doubt as to its subject; but "as the subject of the third pursues not as a robber, but as intent on a matrimonial alliance," he will in the end have no grudge against him.

5. "The good fortune falling to the fifth line, yin," affords occasion for joy.

6. "The freedom from error attached to the subject of the topmost line, with no ornament but the simple white," shows how he has attained his aim.

FROM THE NOTES OF JAMES LEGGE:

Pi is the symbol both of what is ornamental and of

the act of adorning. As there is ornament in nature, so should there be in society; but its place is secondary to what is substantial. This is the view of king Wen.

Line 2, yin, and Line 3, yang, are both in their proper places. These two, therefore, keep together and are as the beard and the chin: what is substantial commands and rules what is merely ornamental. Ornament recognizes the superiority of solidity.

A return to pure, "white," simplicity shows substantiality is better than ornament. Being clothed in simple white crowns the lesson that ornament must be kept in a secondary place.

The "ornamental figures in the sky" are all the heavenly bodies in their relative positions and various movements, producing day and night, heat and cold. The observances of society are the ceremonies and performances which regulate and beautify the intercourse of men, and constitute the transforming lessons of sagely wisdom.

"A mountain," says Cheng K'ang Ch'eng, "is a place where we find grass, trees, and a hundred other things. A fire burning below it throws up its light, and brings them all out in beauty; and this gives the idea of ornament, or being ornamented. The various processes of government are small matters, and elegance and ornament help their course. But great matters of judgment demand the simple, unornamented truth."

KEN, MOUNTAIN
over
K'UN, EARTH

23 Po; Overthrow

THE TEXT:

Po indicates that in the state which it symbolizes it will not be advantageous to make a movement in any direction whatever.

1. The first line, yin, shows one overturning the couch by injuring its legs. The injury will go on to the destruction of all firm correctness, and there will be evil.

2. The second line, yin, shows one overthrowing the couch by injuring its frame. The injury will go on to the destruction of all firm correctness, and there will be evil.

3. The third line, yin, shows its subject among the overthrowers; but there will be no error.

4. The fourth line, yin, shows its subject having overthrown the couch, and going to injure the skin of him who lies on it. There will be evil.

5. The fifth line, yin, shows its subject leading on the others like a string of fishes, and obtaining for them the favor that lights on the inmates of the palace. There will be advantage in every way.

6. The topmost line, yang, shows its subject as a great fruit which has not been eaten. The superior man finds the people again as a chariot carrying him. The small men by their course overthrow their own dwellings.

FROM THE WINGS:

Po denotes overthrowing or being overthrown. We see the yin lines threatening to change the last yang line into one of themselves.

That "it will not be advantageous to make a movement in any direction whatever" appears from the fact that the small men are now growing and increasing. The superior man acts according to the exigency of the time, and stops all forward movement, looking at the significance of the trigrams. He values the processes of decrease and increase, of fullness and decadence, as seen in the movements of the heavenly bodies.

The trigrams representing Earth and above it that for Mountain, which adheres to the earth, form Po. Superiors, in accordance with this, seek to strengthen those below them, to secure the peace and stability of their own position.

1. "He overthrows the couch by injuring its legs": thus he commences his work of ruin with what is lowest in the superior man.

2. "He destroys the couch by injuring its frame": the superior man has as yet no associates.

3. That "there will be no error on the part of this one among the overthrowers" arises from the difference between him and the others above and below.

4. "He has overthrown the couch, and proceeds to injure the skin of him who lies on it": calamity is very near at hand.

5. "He obtains for them the favor that lights on the inmates of the palace": in the end there will be no grudge against him.

6. "The superior man finds himself in a carriage": he is carried along by the people. "The small men by

their course overthrow their own dwellings": they can never again be of use to them.

FROM THE NOTES OF JAMES LEGGE:

Po is the symbol of falling or causing to fall; the process of decay, or overthrow.

The symbolism is chiefly that of a couch with its occupant. The idea of the hexagram requires this occupant to be overthrown, or at least that an attempt be made to overthrow him. The object of the evil worker is the overthrow of all firm correctness. Of course there will be evil.

The symbolic figures in the hexagram are K'un, the representative of docility, acting as circumstances require, and Ken, the representative of Mountain, which arrests the progress of the traveler. The superior man of the topmost line thus interprets them, and acts accordingly. Yet he is not without hope. Night is succeeded by day; the moon wanes, and then begins to wax again. So will it be in life. As we read in the Hebrew prophet Isaiah, "In returning and rest shall ye be saved; in quietness and confidence shall be your strength."

K'UN, EARTH
over
CHEN, THUNDER

24 Fu; Returning

THE TEXT:

Fu indicates that there will be free course and progress in what it denotes. The subject of it finds no one to distress him in his exits and entrances; friends come to him, and no error is committed. He will return and repeat his proper course. In seven days comes his return. There will be advantage in whatever direction movement is made.

1. The first line, yang, shows its subject returning from an error of no great extent, which would not proceed to anything requiring repentance. There will be great good fortune.

2. The second line, yin, shows the admirable return of its subject. There will be good fortune.

3. The third line, yin, shows one who has made repeated returns. The position is perilous, but there will be no error.

4. The fourth line, yin, shows its subject moving right in the center among those represented by the other yin lines, and yet returning alone to his proper path.

5. The fifth line, yin, shows the noble return of its subject. There will be no ground for repentance.

6. The topmost line, yin, shows its subject all astray on the subject of returning. There will be evil. There

will be calamities and errors. If with his views he put the hosts in motion, the end will be a great defeat, whose issues will extend to the ruler of the state. Even in ten years he will not be able to repair the disaster.

FROM THE WINGS:

"Fu indicates the free course and progress of what it denotes": it is the coming back of what is intended by the undivided yang line.

Its subject's actions show movement directed by accordance with natural order. Hence "he finds no one to distress him in his exits and entrances," and "friends come to him, and no error is committed."

"He will return and repeat his proper course; in seven days comes his return": such is the movement of the heavenly revolution.

"There will be advantage in whatever direction movement is made": the strong lines are growing and increasing.

Do we not see in Fu the mind of heaven and earth?

The trigram representing the earth and that for thunder in the midst of it form Fu. The ancient kings, in accordance with this, on the day of the winter solstice, shut the gates of the passes from one state to another, so that the traveling merchants could not then pursue their journeys, nor the princes go on with the inspection of their states.

1. "Returning from an error of no great extent" is the prelude to the cultivation of the person.

2. "The good fortune attendant on the admirable return of the subject of the second line" is due to his condescension to the virtuous subject of the line below.

3. Notwithstanding "the perilous position of him who

has made many returns," there will be no error through his aiming after righteousness.

4. "He moves right in the center among those represented by the other yin lines, and yet returns alone": his object is to pursue the proper path.

5. "The noble return, giving no ground for repentance," is due to the subject of the line striving to perfect himself in accordance with his central position.

6. "The evil consequent on being all astray on the subject of returning" is because the course pursued is contrary to the proper course for a ruler.

FROM THE NOTES OF JAMES LEGGE:

Fu symbolizes the idea of returning, coming back or over again. The last hexagram showed us inferior prevailing over superior men, all that is good in nature and society yielding before what is bad. But change is the law of nature and society. When decay has reached its climax, recovery will begin to take place.

"Thunder in the midst of the earth" is thunder shut up and silent, just able to make its presence felt. So is it with the first genial stirrings of life after the winter solstice; so is it with the first returning steps of the wanderer to virtue. As the spring of life has to be nursed in quietness, so also has the purpose of good. The ancient statutes here referred to must have been like the present cessation from public and private business at the time of the new year, when all the Chinese people are for a time dissolved in festivity and joy.

"The mind of heaven and earth" is the love of life and of all goodness that rules in the course of nature and providence.

CH'IEN, HEAVEN
over
CHEN, THUNDER

25 Wu Wang; Sincerity

THE TEXT:

Wu Wang indicates great progress and success. There will be advantage in being firm and correct. If its subject and his action be not correct, he will fall into errors and it will not be advantageous for him to move in any direction.

1. The first line, yang, shows its subject free from all insincerity. His advance will be accompanied with good fortune.

2. The second line, yin, shows one who reaps without having plowed, and gathers the produce of his third year's fields without having cultivated them the first year for that end. To such a one there will be advantage in whatever direction he may move.

3. The third line, yin, shows calamity happening to one who is free from insincerity; as in the case of an ox that has been tied up. A passerby finds it and carries it off, while the people in the neighborhood have the calamity of being accused and apprehended.

4. The fourth line, yang, shows a case in which, if its subject can remain firm and correct, there will be no error.

5. The fifth line, yang, shows one who is free from insincerity, and yet has fallen ill. Let him not use medicine, and he will have occasion for joy in his recovery.

6. The topmost line, yang, shows its subject free from insincerity, yet sure to fall into error, if he take action. His action will not be advantageous in any way.

FROM THE WINGS:

In Wu Wang we have the attributes of motive power and strength; we have the yang line of the fifth place in the central position, and responded to by the yin second: there will be "great progress proceeding from correctness; such is the appointment of Heaven.

"If its subject and his action be not correct, he will fall into errors, and it will not be advantageous for him to move in any direction": whither can he who thinks he is free from all insincerity, and yet is as here described proceed? Can anything be done advantageously by him whom the will and appointment of Heaven do not help?

The thunder rolls all under the sky, and to everything there is given its nature, free from all insincerity. The ancient kings, in accordance with this, made their regulations in complete accordance with the seasons, thereby nourishing all things.

1. When "he who is free from insincerity makes any movement," he will get what he desires.

2. "He reaps without having plowed": the thought of riches to be got had not risen in his mind.

3. "The passerby gets the ox": this proves a calamity to the people of the neighborhood.

4. "If he can remain firm and correct there will be no error": he firmly holds fast his correctness.

5. "Medicine in the case of one who is free from insincerity!" it should not be tried at all.

6. "The action in this case of one who is free from insincerity will occasion the calamity arising from action when the time for it is exhausted."

FROM THE NOTES OF JAMES LEGGE:

Wang is the symbol of being reckless, and often of being insincere; Wu Wang is descriptive of a state of entire freedom from such a condition; its subject is one who is entirely simple and sincere. The quality is characteristic of the action of Heaven, and of the highest style of humanity. In this hexagram we have an essay on this noble attribute. An absolute rectitude is essential to it. The nearer one comes to the idea of the quality, the more powerful will be his influence, the greater his success. But let him see to it that he never swerves from being correct.

KEN, MOUNTAIN
over
CH'IEN, HEAVEN

26 TA CH'U; GREAT ACCUMULATION

THE TEXT:

Under the conditions of Ta Ch'u it will be advantageous to be firm and correct. If its subject do not seek to enjoy his revenues in his own family without doing service at court, there will be good fortune. It will be advantageous for him to cross the great stream.

1. The first line, yang, shows its subject in a position of peril. It will be advantageous for him to stop his advance.

2. The second line, yang, shows a carriage with the strap under it removed.

3. The third line, yang, shows its subject urging his way with good horses. It will be advantageous for him to realize the difficulty of his course, and to be firm and correct, exercising himself daily in his charioteering and methods of defense; then there will be advantage in whatever direction he may advance.

4. The fourth line, yin, shows the young bull, and yet having the piece of wood over his horns. There will be great good fortune.

5. The fifth line, yin, shows the teeth of a castrated hog. There will be good fortune.

6. The sixth line, yang, shows its subject as in command of the firmament of heaven. There will be progress.

FROM THE WINGS:

In the trigrams composing Ta Ch'u we have the attributes of the greatest strength and of substantial solidity, which emit a brilliant light and indicate a daily renewal of virtue.

The strong line is in the highest place, and suggests the value set on talents and virtue; there is power in the upper trigram to keep the strongest in restraint: all this shows "the great correctness" required in the hexagram.

"The good fortune attached to the subject's not seeking to enjoy his revenues in his own family" shows how talents and virtue are nourished.

"It will be advantageous to cross the great stream": the fifth line, representing the ruler, is responded to by the second, the central line of Ch'ien, representing Heaven.

The trigram representing a mountain, and in the midst of it that representing heaven, form Ta Ch'u. The superior man, in accordance with this, stores largely in his memory the words and deeds of former men, to serve the accumulation of his virtue.

1. "He is in a position of peril; it will be advantageous for him to stop his advance": he should not rashly expose himself to calamity.

2. "He is as a carriage from which the strap under it has been removed": being in the central position, he will incur no blame.

3. "There will be advantage in whatever direction he may advance": the subject of the topmost line is of the same mind with him.

4. "The great good fortune indicated by the fourth line, yin," shows that there is occasion for joy.

5. "The good fortune indicated by the fifth line, yin," shows that there is occasion for congratulation.

6. "In command of the firmament of heaven": the way is grandly open for movement.

FROM THE NOTES OF JAMES LEGGE:

"The symbol of heaven in the midst of a mountain forms Ta Ch'u. The superior man, in accordance with this, stores largely in his memory the words of former men and their conduct, to serve the accumulation of his virtue." We are ready to exclaim and ask, "Heaven, the sky, in the midst of a mountain! Can there be such a thing?" and Chu Hsi will tell us in reply, "No, there cannot be such a thing in reality; but you can conceive it for the purpose of the symbolism."

Ch'u has two meanings. It is the symbol of restraint and of accumulation. What is repressed and restrained accumulates its strength and increases its volume. Both these meanings are found in the treatise on the T'uan. The different lines are occupied with the repression or restraint of movement. The first three lines receive that repression, the upper three exercise it. The accumulation to which all tends is that of virtue; and hence the name of Ta Ch'u, "the Great Accumulation."

What the T'uan teaches is that he who goes about to accumulate his virtue must be firm and correct and may then, engaging in the public service, enjoy the king's grace, and undertake the most difficult enterprises.

The young bull in line 4 has not yet got horns. The attaching to their rudiments the piece of wood to prevent him from goring is an instance of extraordinary precaution; and precaution is always good.

Ta Ch'u evidently means the "grand accumulation"

of virtue, indicated by the attributes of its component trigrams. "Substantial solidity" may very well be given as the attribute of mountains.

In a kingdom where the object of the government is the accumulation of virtue, good and able men will not be left in obscurity.

KEN, MOUNTAIN
over
CHEN, THUNDER

27 I; NOURISHMENT

FROM THE TEXT:

I indicates that with firm correctness there will be good fortune in what is denoted by it. We must look at what we are seeking to nourish, and by the exercise of our thoughts seek for the proper sustenance.

1. The first line, yang, seems to be thus addressed, "You leave your efficacious tortoise, and look at me till your lower jaw hangs down." There will be evil.

2. The second line, yin, shows one looking downward for nourishment, which is contrary to what is proper; or seeking it from the height above, advance toward which will lead to evil.

3. The third line, yin, shows one acting contrary to the method of nourishing. However firm he may be, there will be evil. For ten years let him not take any action, for it will not be in any way advantageous.

4. The fourth line, yin, shows one looking downward for the power to nourish. There will be good fortune. Looking with a tiger's downward unwavering glare, and with his desire that impels him to spring after spring, he will fall into no error.

5. The fifth line, yin, shows one acting contrary to what is regular and proper; but if he abide in firmness, there will be good fortune. He should not, however, try to cross the great stream.

6. The sixth line, yang, shows him from whom comes the nourishing. His position is perilous, but there will be good fortune. It will be advantageous to cross the great stream.

FROM THE WINGS:

"I indicates that with firm correctness there will be good fortune": when the nourishing is correct, there will be good fortune. "We must look at what we are seeking to nourish": we must look at those whom we wish to nourish. "We must by the exercise of our thoughts seek the proper food": we must look to our own nourishing of ourselves.

Heaven and earth nourish all things. The sages nourish men of talents and virtue, through them to reach to the myriads of the people. Great is the work intended by this nourishing in its time!

The trigram representing a mountain and under it that for thunder form I. The superior man, in accordance with this, enjoins watchfulness over our words, and the temperate regulation of our eating and drinking.

1. "You look at me till your lower jaw hangs down": the subject of the line is thus shown unfit to be thought noble.

2. "The evil of advance by the subject of the second line, yin," is owing to his leaving in his movements his proper associates.

3. "For ten years let him not take any action": his course is greatly opposed to what is right.

4. "The good fortune attached to looking downward for the power to nourish," shows how brilliant will be the diffusion of that power from the subject of the line's superior position.

5. "The good fortune from abiding in firmness" is due to the docility of the subject of the line in following the subject of the line above.

6. "The good fortune, notwithstanding the peril of his position, of him from whom comes the nourishing," affords great cause for congratulation.

FROM THE NOTES OF JAMES LEGGE:

I is the symbol of the upper jaw and gives name to the hexagram; but the whole figure suggests the appearance of the mouth. There are the two undivided lines at the bottom and top and the four divided lines between them. The first line is the first in the trigram Chen, denoting movement; and the sixth is the third in Ken, denoting what is solid. The former is the lower jaw, part of the mobile chin; and the other the more fixed upper jaw. The open lines are the cavity of the mouth. As the name of the hexagram, I denotes nourishing—one's body or mind, one's self or others. The nourishment in both the matter and method will differ according to the object of it; and every one must determine what to employ and do in every case by exercising his own thoughts, only one thing being premised —that in both respects the nourishing must be correct and in harmony with what is right. The auspice of the whole hexagram is good.

TUI, MARSH
over
SUN, WIND

28 TA KUO; GREATNESS AND DIFFICULTY

THE TEXT:

Ta Kuo suggests to us a beam that is weak. There will be advantage in moving under its conditions in any direction whatever; there will be success.

1. The first line, yin, shows one placing mats of the white mao grass under things set on the ground. There will be no error.

2. The second line, yang, shows a decayed willow producing shoots, or an old husband in possession of his young wife. There will be advantage in every way.

3. The third line, yang, shows a beam that is weak. There will be evil.

4. The fourth line, yang, shows a beam curving upward. There will be good fortune. If the subject of it looks for other help but that of line 1, there will be cause for regret.

5. The fifth line, yang, shows a decayed willow producing flowers, or an old wife in possession of her young husband. There will be occasion neither for blame nor for praise.

6. The topmost line, yin, shows its subject with extraordinary boldness wading through a stream, till the water hides the crown of his head. There will be evil, but no ground for blame.

198

FROM THE WINGS:

Ta Kuo shows yang lines in excess.

In "the beam that is weak" we see weakness both in the lowest and the topmost lines.

The strong lines are in excess, but two of them are in the central positions. The action of the hexagram is represented by the symbols of flexibility and satisfaction. Hence it is said, "There will be advantage in moving in any direction whatever; there will be success."

Great indeed is the work to be done in this very extraordinary time.

The trigram representing trees hidden beneath that for the waters of a marsh forms Ta Kuo. The superior man, accordingly with this, stands up alone and has no fear, and keeps retired from the world without regret.

1. "He places mats of the white mao grass under things set on the ground": he feels his weakness and his being in the lowest place and uses extraordinary care.

2. "An old husband and a young wife": such association is extraordinary.

3. "The evil connected with the beam that is weak" arises from this, that no help can be given to the condition thus represented.

4. "The good fortune connected with the beam curving upward" arises from this, that it does not bend toward what is below.

5. "A decayed willow produces flowers": but how can this secure its long continuance? "An old wife and a young husband": this also is a thing to be ashamed of.

6. "Evil follows wading with extraordinary boldness through the stream": but the act affords no ground for blame.

FROM THE NOTES OF JAMES LEGGE:

Very extraordinary times require very extraordinary gifts in the conduct of affairs in them. This is the text on which king Wen and his son discourse after their fashion in this hexagram. What goes, in their view, to constitute anything extraordinary is its greatness and difficulty.

"Wood" appears as the natural object symbolized by Sun, and not "wind," which we find more commonly. The attribute of "flexibility," however, is the quality of Sun, whether used of wind or of wood.

K'AN, WATER
Repeated

29   K'AN; DANGER

THE TEXT:

K'an, here repeated, shows the possession of sincerity, through which the mind is penetrating. Action in accordance with this will be of high value.

1. The first line, yin, shows its subject in the double defile, and yet entering a cavern within it. There will be evil.

2. The second line, yang, shows its subject in all the peril of the defile. He will, however, get a little of the deliverance that he seeks.

3. The third line, yin, shows its subject, whether he comes or goes, descends or ascends, confronted by a defile. All is peril to him and unrest. His endeavors will lead him into the cavern of the pit. There should be no action in such a case.

4. The fourth line, yin, shows its subject at a feast, with a bottle of spirits and a basket of rice; the cups and bowls are only of earthenware. He introduces his important lessons as his ruler's intelligence admits. There will in the end be no error.

5. The fifth line, yang, shows the water of the defile not yet full, so that it might flow away; but order will soon be brought about. There will be no error.

6. The topmost line, yin, shows its subject bound with cords of three strands or two strands, and placed in the

thicket of thorns. But in three years he does not learn the course for him to pursue. There will be evil.

FROM THE WINGS:

K'an repeated shows us one defile succeeding another.

This is the nature of water; it flows on without accumulating its volume. It pursues its way through a dangerous defile without losing its true nature.

That "the mind is penetrating" is indicated by the yang line in the center. That "action in accordance with this will be of high value" tells us that advance will be followed by achievement.

The dangerous height of heaven cannot be ascended; the difficult places of the earth are mountains, rivers, hills, and mounds. Kings and princes arrange, by means of such strengths, to maintain their territories. Great indeed is the use of what is here taught about seasons of peril.

The representation of water flowing on continuously forms the repeated K'an. The superior man, in accordance with this, maintains constantly the virtue of his heart and the integrity of his conduct, and practices the business of instruction.

1. "In the double defile, he enters a cavern within it": he has missed his proper way, and there will be evil.

2. "He will get a little of the deliverance that he seeks": he will not yet escape from his environment.

3. "Whether he comes or goes, he is confronted by a defile": he will never in such circumstances achieve any success.

4. "Nothing but a bottle of spirits and a subsidiary basket of rice": these describe the meeting at this point of those who are represented by the yang and yin lines.

5. "The water in the defile is not full so as to flow away": the virtue indicated by the central situation is not yet sufficiently great.

6. "The sixth line shows its subject missing his proper course": "there will be evil for three years."

FROM THE NOTES OF JAMES LEGGE:

The trigram K'an, which is doubled to form this hexagram, is the lineal symbol of water. Its meaning, as a character, is "a pit," "a perilous cavity, or defile"; and here and elsewhere in the I it leads the reader to think of a dangerous defile, with water flowing through it. It becomes symbolic of danger, and what the authors of the Text had in mind was to show how danger should be encountered, its effect on the mind, and how to get out of it.

The trigram exhibits a strong central line, between two divided lines. The central represented to king Wen the sincere honesty and goodness of the subject of the hexagram, whose mind was sharpened and made penetrating by contact with danger. and who acted in a manner worthy of his character. It is implied, though the T'uan does not say it, that he would get out of the danger.

Liang Yin says: "Water stops at the proper time, and moves at the proper time. Is not this an emblem of the course of the superior man in dealing with danger?"

On paragraph 4 the K'ang Hsi editors say that to exercise one's self in meeting difficulty and peril is the way to establish and strengthen the character, and that the use of such experience is seen in all measures for self-defense, there being no helmet and mail like loyalty and good faith, and no shield and tower like propriety and righteousness.

LI, FIRE
Repeated

30 Li; Double Brightness

THE TEXT:

Li indicates that in regard to what it denotes, it will be advantageous to be firm and correct, and that thus there will be free course and success. Let its subject also nourish a docility like that of the cow, and there will be good fortune.

1. The first line, yang, shows one ready to move with confused steps. But he treads at the same time reverently, and there will be no mistake.

2. The second line, yin, shows its subject in his place in yellow. There will be great good fortune.

3. The third line, yang, shows its subject in a position like that of the declining sun. Instead of playing on his instrument of earthenware, and singing to it, he utters the groans of an old man of eighty. There will be evil.

4. The fourth line, yang, shows the manner of its subject's coming. How abrupt it is, as with fire, with death, to be rejected by all!

5. The fifth line, yin, shows its subject as one with tears flowing in torrents, and groaning in sorrow. There will be good fortune.

6. The topmost line, yang, shows the king employing its subject in his punitive expeditions. Achieving admirable merit, he breaks only the chiefs of the rebels. Where his prisoners were not their associates, he does not punish. There will be no error.

FROM THE WINGS:

Li means being attached to. The sun and moon have their place in the sky. All the grains, grass, and trees have their place on the earth. The double brightness of the two trigrams adheres to what is correct, and the result is the transforming and perfecting all under the sky.

The second line, yin, occupies the middle and correct position, and gives the indication of "a free and successful course"; and, moreover, "nourishing docility like that of the cow" will lead to good fortune.

The trigram for brightness, repeated, forms Li. The great man, in accordance with this, cultivates more and more his brilliant virtue, and diffuses its brightness over the four quarters of the land.

1. "The reverent attention directed to his confused steps" is the way by which error is avoided.

2. "The great good fortune from the subject of the second line occupying his place in yellow" is owing to his holding the course of the due mean.

3. "A position like that of the declining sun": how can it continue long?

4. "How abrupt is the manner of his coming!" None can bear with him.

5. "The good fortune attached to the fifth line, yin," is due to its occupying the place of a king or a prince.

6. "The king employs him in his punitive expeditions": the object is to bring the regions to a correct state.

FROM THE NOTES OF JAMES LEGGE:

Li is the name of the trigram representing fire and light, and the sun as the source of both of these. Its virtue or attribute is brightness, and by a natural meta-.

phor intelligence. But Li has also the meaning of in-hering in, or adhering to, being attached to. Both these significations occur in connection with the hexagram, and make it difficult to determine what was the subject of it in the minds of the authors. If we take the whole figure as expressing the subject, we have, as in the treatise on the T'uan, "a double brightness," a phrase which is understood to denominate the ruler. If we take the two central lines as indicating the subject, we have weakness, dwelling with strength above and below. In either case there are required from the subject a strict adherence to what is correct, and a docile humility. Cheng K'ang Ch'eng says: "The nature of the ox is docile, and that of the cow is much more so. The sub-ject of the hexagram adhering closely to what is correct, he must be able to act in obedience to it, as docile as a cow, and then there will be good fortune."

"The double brightness" has been much discussed. Some say that it means "the ruler," becoming brighter and brighter. Others say that it means both the ruler and his ministers, combining their brightness. The former view seems to me the better.

TUI, MARSH
over
KEN, MOUNTAIN

31   HSIEN; MUTUAL INFLUENCE

THE TEXT:

Hsien indicates that, on the fulfillment of the conditions implied in it, there will be free course and success. Its advantageousness will depend on being firm and correct, as in marrying a young lady. There will be good fortune.

1. The first line, yin, shows one moving his great toes.

2. The second line, yin, shows one moving the calves of his leg. There will be evil. If he abide quiet in his place, there will be food fortune.

3. The third line, yang, shows one moving his thighs, and keeping close hold of those whom he follows. Going forward in this way will cause regret.

4. The fourth line, yang, shows that firm correctness which will lead to good fortune, and prevent all occasion for repentance. If its subject be unsettled in his movements, only his friends will follow his purpose.

5. The fifth line, yang, shows one moving the flesh along the spine above the heart. There will be no occasion for repentance.

6. The sixth line, yin, shows one moving his jaws and tongue.

FROM THE WINGS:

Hsien is here used in the meaning of mutually influencing.

The weak trigram above, and the strong one below; their two influences moving and responding to each other, and thereby forming a union; the repression of the one and the satisfaction of the other; with their relative position, where the male is placed below the female: all these things convey the notion of "a free and successful course on the fulfillment of the conditions, while the advantage will depend on being firm and correct, as in marrying a young lady, and there will be good fortune."

Heaven and earth exert their influences, and there ensue the transformation and production of all things. The sages influence the minds of men, and the result is harmony and peace all under the sky. If we look at the method and issues of those influences, the true character of heaven and earth and of all things can be seen.

The trigram representing a mountain and above it that for the waters of a marsh form Hsien. The superior man, in accordance with this, keeps his mind free from preoccupation, and open to receive the influences of others.

1. "He moves his great toe": his mind is set on what is beyond himself.

2. Though "there would be evil; yet, if he abide quiet in his place, there will be good fortune": through compliance with the circumstances of his condition and place there will be no injury.

3. "He moves his thighs": he still does not want to rest in his place. His will is set on "following others": what he holds in his grasp is low.

4. "Firm correctness will lead to good fortune, and prevent all occasion for repentance": there has not yet been any harm from a selfish wish to influence. "He is unsettled in his movements": his power to influence is not yet either brilliant or great.

5. "He tries to move the flesh along the spine above the heart": his aim is trivial.

6. "He moves his jaws and tongue": he only talks with loquacious mouth.

FROM THE NOTES OF JAMES LEGGE:

In various ways the waters of a marsh, placed high above the adjacent land, will descend to water and fertilize them. This symbolism agrees sufficiently well with the idea of influence passing between a superior and inferior party in relation with each other. The application of the symbolism is sufficiently appropriate. The commentators see in it especially the lesson of humility—emptiness of self, or poverty of spirit—in order that the influences to which we are subjected may have free course.

Coming now to the figure, and its lines, the subject is that of mutual influence; and the author teaches that that influence, correct in itself and for correct ends, is sure to be effective. He gives an instance, the case of a man marrying a young lady, the regulations for which have been laid down in China from the earliest times with great strictness and particularity. Such influence will be effective and fortunate.

CHEN, THUNDER
over
SUN, WIND

32   HENG; PERSEVERANCE

THE TEXT:

Heng indicates successful progress and no error in what it denotes. But the advantage will come from being firm and correct; movement in any direction whatever will be advantageous.

1. The first line, yin, shows its subject deeply desirous of long continuance. Even with firm correctness there will be evil; there will be no advantage in any way.

2. The second line, yang, shows all occasion for repentance disappearing.

3. The third line, yang, shows one who does not continuously maintain his virtue. There are those who will impute this to him as a disgrace. However firm he may be, there will be ground for regret.

4. The fourth line, yang, shows a field where there is no game.

5. The fifth line, yin, shows its subject continuously maintaining the virtue indicated by it. In a wife this will be fortunate; in a husband, evil.

6. The topmost line, yin, shows its subject exciting himself to long continuance. There will be evil.

FROM THE WINGS:

Heng denotes long continuance. The strong trigram

is above and the weak one below; they are the symbols of thunder and wind, which are in mutual communication; they have the qualities of docility and motive force; these things are all found in Heng.

When it is said that "Heng indicates successful progress and no error in what it denotes; but the advantage will come from being firm and correct," this indicates that there must be long continuance in its way of operation. The way of heaven and earth is to be long continued in their operation without stopping.

When it is said that "Movement in any direction whatever will be advantageous," this implies that when the moving power is spent, it will begin again.

The sun and moon, realizing in themselves the course of Heaven, can perpetuate their shining. The four seasons, by their changing and transforming, can perpetuate their production of things. The sages persevere long in their course, and all under the sky are transformed and perfect. When we look at what they continue doing long, the natural tendencies of heaven, earth, and all things can be seen.

The trigram representing thunder and that for wind form Heng. The superior man, in accordance with this, stands firm, and does not change his method of operation.

1. "The evil attached to the deep desire for long continuance in the subject of the first line" arises from the deep seeking for it at the commencement of things.

2. "All occasion for repentance on the part of the subject of the second line, yang, disappears": he can abide long in the due mean.

3. "He does not continuously maintain his virtue": nowhere will he be borne with.

4. Going for long to what is not his proper place, how can he get game?

5. "Such firm correctness in a wife will be fortunate": it is hers to the end of life to follow with an unchanged mind. The husband must decide what is right and lay down the rule accordingly: for him to follow like a wife is evil.

6. "The subject of the topmost line is exciting himself to long continuance": far will he be from achieving merit.

FROM THE NOTES OF JAMES LEGGE:

The subject of this hexagram may be given as perseverance in well doing, or in continuously acting out the law of one's being.

All the conditions must be understood as leading to the indication of progress and success, which is illustrated by the analogy of the course of heaven and earth.

"Movement in any direction" indicates the ever-occurring new modes and spheres of activity, to which he who is firm and correct is called.

CH'IEN, HEAVEN
over
KEN, MOUNTAIN

33 TUN; SECLUSION

THE TEXT:

Tun indicates successful progress in its circumstances. To a small extent it will still be advantageous to be firm and correct.

1. The first line, yin, shows a retiring tail. The position is perilous. No movement in any direction should be made.

2. The second line, yin, shows its subject holding his purpose fast as if by a thong made from the hide of a yellow ox, which cannot be broken.

3. The third line, yang, shows one retiring but bound, to his distress and peril. If he were to deal with his binders as in nourishing a servant or concubine, it would be fortunate for him.

4. The fourth line, yang, shows its subject retiring notwithstanding his likings. In a superior man this will lead to good fortune; a small man cannot attain to this.

5. The fifth line, yang, shows its subject retiring in an admirable way. With firm correctness there will be good fortune.

6. The sixth line, yang, shows its subject retiring in a noble way. It will be advantageous in every respect.

FROM THE WINGS:

"Tun indicates successful progress": that is, in the

very retiring which Tun denotes there is such progress. The yang line is in the ruling place, the fifth, and is properly responded to by the second line, yin. The action takes place according to the requirement of the time.

"To a small extent it will still be advantageous to be firm and correct": the small men are gradually encroaching and advancing.

Great indeed is the significance of what is required to be done in the time that necessitates retiring.

The trigram representing the sky and below it that for a mountain form Tun. The superior man, in accordance with this, keeps small men at a distance, not by showing that he hates them, but by his own dignified gravity.

1. There is "the perilousness of the position shown by the retiring tail": but if "no movement" be made, what disaster can there be?

2. "He holds it as by a thong from the hide of a yellow ox": his purpose is firm.

3. "The peril connected with the case of one retiring, though bound," is due to the consequent distress and exhaustion. "If he were to deal as in nourishing a servant or concubine, it would be fortunate for him": but a great affair cannot be dealt with in this way.

4. "A superior man retires notwithstanding his likings; a small man cannot attain to this."

5. "He retires in an admirable way, and with firm correctness there will be good fortune": this is due to the rectitude of his purpose.

6. "He retires in a noble way, and his doing so will be advantageous in every respect": he who does so has no doubts about his course.

FROM THE NOTES OF JAMES LEGGE:

Tun is the hexagram of the sixth month; the yin influence is represented by two divided lines, and has made good its footing in the year. The figure thus suggested to king Wen the growth of small and unprincipled men in the state, before whose advance superior men were obliged to retire. This is the theme of his essay: "when small men multiply and increase in power, the necessity of the time requires superior men to withdraw before them." Yet the auspice of Tun is not all bad. By firm correctness the threatened evil may be arrested to a small extent.

"A retiring tail" seems to suggest the idea of the subject of the lines hurrying away, which would only aggravate the evil and danger of the time.

"The superior man," it is said, "advances or withdraws according to the character of the time. The strength and correct position of the fifth line show that he is able to maintain himself; and as it is responded to by the weak second line, no opposition to what is correct in him would come from any others. He might therefore keep his place; but looking at lines 1 and 2 he recognizes in them the advance and irrepressible progress of small men. For a time it is better for him to give way and withdraw from the field. Thus there is successful progress even in his retiring."

CHEN, THUNDER
over
CH'IEN, HEAVEN

34 Ta Chuang; Abundant Strength

The Text:

Ta Chuang indicates that under the conditions which it symbolizes it will be advantageous to be firm and correct.

1. The first line, yang, shows its subject manifesting his strength in his toes. But advance will lead to evil, most certainly.

2. The second line, yang, shows that with firm correctness there will be good fortune.

3. The third line, yang, shows, in the case of a small man, one using all his strength; and in the case of a superior man, one whose rule is not to do so. Even with firm correctness the position would be perilous. The exercise of strength in it might be compared to the case of a ram butting against a fence and getting his horns entangled.

4. The fourth line, yang, shows a case in which firm correctness leads to good fortune, and occasion for repentance disappears. We see the fence opened without the horns being entangled. The strength is like that in the wheelspokes of a large wagon.

5. The fifth line, yin, shows one who loses his ram-like strength in the ease of his position. But there will be no occasion for repentance.

6. The sixth line, yin, shows one who may be compared to the ram butting against the fence, and unable either to retreat or to advance. There will not be advantage in any respect; but if he realize the difficulty of his position, there will be good fortune.

FROM THE WINGS:

In Ta Chuang we see that which is great becoming strong. We have the trigram denoting strength directing that which denotes movement, and hence the whole is expressive of vigor.

"Ta Chuang indicates that it will be advantageous to be firm and correct": that which is great should be correct. Given correctness and greatness in their highest degree, the character and tendencies of heaven and earth can be seen.

The trigram representing Heaven and above it that for Thunder form Ta Chuang. The superior man, in accordance with this, does not take a step which is not according to propriety.

1. "He manifests his vigor in his toes": this will certainly lead to exhaustion.

2. "The second line, yang, shows that with firm correctness there will be good fortune": this is due to its being in the center and its subjects exemplifying the due mean.

3. "The small man uses all his strength; in the case of the superior man it is his rule not to do so."

4. "The fence is opened and the horns are not entangled": the subject of the line still advances.

5. "He loses his ram and hardly perceives it": he is not in his appropriate place.

6. "He is unable either to retreat or to advance":

this is owing to his want of care. "If he realizes the difficulty of his position, there will be good fortune": his error will not be prolonged.

FROM THE NOTES OF JAMES LEGGE:

The strong lines predominate in Ta Chuang. It suggested to king Wen a state or condition of things in which there was abundance of strength and vigor. Was strength alone enough for the conduct of affairs? No. He saw also in the figure that which suggested to him that strength should be held in subordination to the idea of right and exerted only in harmony with it.

In illustration of the symbolism of the trigrams here, Cheng K'ang Ch'eng says well: "Thunder rolling above in the sky and making all things shake is the emblem of great power." In passing on to its application he starts with a beautiful saying of antiquity, that "the strong man is he who overcomes himself." That this thought was in the mind of the writer I can well believe; but the analogy between the natural and the moral and spiritual worlds in passing from the phenomenon of thunder to this truth is a thing to be felt, and that can hardly be described.

LI, FIRE
over
K'UN, EARTH

35 CHIN; ADVANCING

THE TEXT:

In Chin we see a prince who secures the tranquility of the people presented with numerous horses by the king, and three times in a day received at interviews.

1. The first line, yin, shows one wishing to advance, and at the same time kept back. Let him be firm and correct, and there will be good fortune. If trust be not reposed in him, let him maintain a large and generous mind, and there will be no error.

2. The second line, yin, shows its subject with the appearance of advancing, and yet of being sorrowful. If he be firm and correct, there will be good fortune. He will receive this great blessing from his grandmother.

3. The third line, yin, shows its subject trusted by all around him. All occasions for repentance will disappear.

4. The fourth line, yang, shows its subject with the appearance of advancing, but like a marmot. However firm and correct he may be, the position is one of peril.

5. The fifth line, yin, shows how all occasion for repentance disappears from its subject. But let him not concern himself about whether he shall fail or succeed. To advance will be fortunate and in every way advantageous.

6. The topmost line, yang, shows one advancing his horns. But he only uses them to punish the rebellious people of his own city. The position is perilous, but there will be good fortune. Yet however firm and correct he may be, there will be occasion for regret.

FROM THE WINGS:

Chin denotes advancing; in Chin we have the bright sun appearing above the earth; the symbol of docile submission cleaving to that of the great brightness; and the yin line advanced and moving above: all these things give us the idea of "a prince who secures the tranquility of the people, presented on that account with numerous horses by the king, and three times in a day received at interviews."

The trigram representing the earth and that for the bright sun coming forth above it form Chin. The superior man, according to this, gives himself to make more brilliant his bright virtue.

1. "He appears wishing to advance, but at the same time being kept back": all alone he pursues the correct course. "Let him maintain a large and generous mind, and there will be no error": he has not yet received an official charge.

2. "He will receive this great blessing": for he is in the central place and the correct position for him.

3. "All around trust him": their common aim is to move upward and act.

4. "He advances like a marmot. However firm and correct he may be, his position is one of peril": his place is not that appropriate for him.

5. "Let him not concern himself whether he fails or succeeds": his movement in advance will afford ground for congratulation.

6. "He uses his horns only to punish the rebellious people of his city": his course of procedure is not yet brilliant.

FROM THE NOTES OF JAMES LEGGE:

The symbolism says he receives it "from his grandmother"; and readers will be startled by the extraordinary statement, as I was when I first read it. Literally the Text says "the king's mother." But "king's father" and "king's mother" are well known Chinese appellations for "grandfather" and "grandmother."

Line 6 is strong, and suggests the idea of its subject to the last continuing his advance, and that not only with firm correctness, but with strong force. The "horns" are an emblem of threatening strength, and though he uses them only in his own state, and against the rebellious there, that such a prince should have any occasion to use force is matter for regret.

K'UN, EARTH
over
LI, FIRE

36 MING I; INTELLIGENCE REPRESSED

THE TEXT:

Ming I indicates that in the circumstances which it denotes it will be advantageous to realize the difficulty of the position and maintain firm correctness.

1. The first line, yang, shows its subject, in the condition indicated by Ming I, flying, but with drooping wings. When the superior man is going away, he may be for three days without eating. Wherever he goes, the people there may speak derisively of him.

2. The second line, yin, shows its subject, in the condition indicated by Ming I, wounded in the left thigh. He saves himself by the strength of a swift horse, and is fortunate.

3. The third line, yang, shows its subject, in the condition indicated by Ming I, hunting in the south, and taking the great chief of the darkness. He should not be eager to make all correct at once.

4. The fourth line, yin, shows its subject just entered into the left side of the belly of the dark land. But he is able to carry out the mind appropriate in the condition indicated by Ming I, quitting the gate and courtyard of the lord of darkness.

5. The fifth line, yin, shows how the count of Chi fulfilled the condition indicated by Ming I. It will be advantageous to be firm and correct.

6. The sixth line, yin, shows the case where there is no light but only obscurity. Its subject had at first ascended to the top of the sky; his future shall be to go into the earth.

FROM THE WINGS:

The symbol of the Earth and that of Brightness entering into the midst of it give the idea of Ming I Brightness wounded or obscured.

The inner trigram denotes being accomplished and bright; the outer, being pliant and submissive. The case of king Wen was that of one who with these qualities was yet involved in great difficulties.

"It will be advantageous to realize the difficulty of the position, and maintain firm correctness": that is, the individual concerned should obscure his brightness. The case of the count of Chi was that of one who, amidst the difficulties of his house, was able thus to maintain his aim and mind correct.

The trigram representing the earth and that for the bright sun entering within it form Ming I. The superior man, in accordance with this, conducts his management of men; he shows his intelligence by keeping it obscured.

1. "The superior man is going away": in such a case he feels it right not to eat.

2. "The good fortune of the subject of the second line, yin," is due to the proper fashion of his acting according to his circumstances.

3. With the aim represented by "hunting in the south" a great achievement is accomplished.

4. "He has just entered into the left side of the belly of the dark land": he is still able to carry out the idea

in his inner mind.

5. "With the firm correctness of the count of Chi, his brightness could not be quite extinguished."

6. "He had at first ascended to the top of the sky": he might have enlightened the four quarters of the kingdom. "His future shall be to go into the earth": he has failed to fulfill the model of a ruler.

FROM THE NOTES OF JAMES LEGGE:

In this hexagram we have the representation of a good and intelligent minister or officer going forward in the service of his country, notwithstanding the occupancy of the throne by a weak and unsympathizing sovereign. Hence comes its name of Ming I, or "Intelligence Wounded," that is, injured and repressed. The treatment of the subject shows how such an officer will conduct himself, and maintain his purpose.

The sun disappearing, as we say, "below the earth," or as the Chinese writer conceives it, "into the midst of . . . earth," sufficiently indicates the obscuration of wounding of brightness—the repression and resistance of the good and bright.

SUN, WIND
over
LI, FIRE

37 CHIA JEN; MEMBERS OF A FAMILY

THE TEXT:

For the realization of what is taught in Chia Jen, or for the regulation of the family, what is most advantageous is that the wife be firm and correct.

1. The first line, yang, shows its subject establishing restrictive regulations in his household. Occasion for repentance will disappear.

2. The second line, yin, shows its subject taking nothing on herself, but in her central place attending to the preparation of the food. Through her firm correctness there will be good fortune.

3. The third line, yang, shows its subject treating the members of the household with stern severity. There will be occasion for repentance, there will be peril, but there will also be good fortune. If the wife and children were to be smirking and chattering, in the end there would be occasion for regret.

4. The fourth line, yin, shows its subject enriching the family. There will be great good fortune.

5. The fifth line, yang, shows the influence of the king extending to his family. There need be no anxiety; there will be good fortune.

6. The topmost line, yang, shows its subject possessed of sincerity and arrayed in majesty. In the end there will be good fortune.

In Chia Jen the wife has her correct place in the inner trigram, and the man his correct place in the outer. That man and woman occupy their correct places is the great righteousness shown in the relation and positions of heaven and earth.

In Chia Jen we have the idea of an authoritative ruler; that, namely, represented by the parental authority.

Let the father be indeed father, and the son son; let the elder brother be indeed elder brother, and the younger brother younger brother; let the husband be indeed husband, and the wife wife: then will the family be in its normal state. Bring the family to that state, and all under heaven will be established.

The trigram representing fire, and that for wind coming forth from it, form Chia Jen. The superior man, in accordance with this, orders his words according to the truth of things, and his conduct so that it is uniformly consistent.

1. "He establishes restrictive regulations in his household": he does so before any change has taken place in their wills.

2. "The good fortune attached to the second line, yin," is due to the docility of its subject, operating with humility.

3. When "the members of the household are treated with stern severity," there has been no great failure in the regulation of the family. When "wife and children are smirking and chattering," the proper economy of the family has been lost.

4. "The family is enriched, and there is great good

fortune": this is due to the docility belonging to the subject of the line, and its being in its correct place.

5. "The influence of the king extends to his family": the intercourse between them is that of mutual love.

6. "The good fortune connected with the display of majesty" describes the result of the recovery of the true character.

FROM THE NOTES OF JAMES LEGGE:

Chia Jen, the name of the hexagram, simply means "a household," or "the members of a family." The subject of the essay based on the figure, however, is the regulation of the family, effected mainly by the cooperation of husband and wife in their several spheres, and only needing to become universal to secure the good order of the kingdom. The important place occupied by the wife in the family is seen in the short sentence of the T'uan. That she be firm and correct, and do her part well, is the first thing necessary to its regulation.

Line 1 is strong and in a strong place. It suggests the necessity of strict rule in governing the family. Regulations must be established and their observance strictly insisted on.

Line 2 is weak and in the proper place for it, the center, moreover, of the lower trigram. It fitly represents the wife and what is said on it tells us of her special sphere and duty; and that she should be unassuming in regard to all beyond her sphere; always being firm and correct.

Line 3 is yang and in an odd place. If the place were central the strength would be tempered; but the subject of the line, in the topmost place of the trigram, may be expected to exceed in severity. But severity is not a bad thing in regulating a family; it is better than laxity and indulgence.

Line 4 is yin and in its proper place. The wife is again suggested to us, and we are told that notwithstanding her being confined to the internal affairs of the household, she can do much to enrich the family.

The subject of the strong fifth line appears as the king. This may be the husband spoken of as also a king; or the real king whose merit is revealed first in his family. The central place here tempers the display of the strength and power.

Line 6 is also strong, and being in an even place, the subject of it might degenerate into stern severity, but he is supposed to be sincere, complete in his personal character and self-culture, and hence his action will only lead to good fortune.

The two trigrams become representative of the family circle and the wide world without it. In the reference to heaven and earth it is not supposed that they are really husband and wife; but in their relation and positions they symbolize that social relation and the individuals in it.

The mention "of mutual love" is unusual in Chinese writings, and must be considered remarkable here. "The husband," says Cheng K'ang Ch'eng, "loves his helpmate in the house; the wife loves him who is the pattern for the family." But however admirable the sentiment is, it comes from the mind of the writer and is not drawn from the Text.

The words of Mencius are aptly quoted in illustration of the lesson: "If a man himself do not walk in the right path, it will not be walked in even by his wife and children."

LI, FIRE
over
TUI, MARSH

38   K'UEI; ALIENATION

THE TEXT:

K'uei indicates that, notwithstanding the condition of things which it denotes, in small matters there will still be good success.

1. The first line, yang, shows that to its subject occasion for repentance will disappear. He has lost his horses, but let him not seek for them; they will return of themselves. Should he meet with bad men, he will not err in communicating with them.

2. The second line, yang, shows its subject happening to meet with his lord in a byway. There will be no error.

3. In the third line, yin, we see one whose carriage is dragged back, while the oxen in it are pushed back, and he is himself subjected to the shaving of his head and the cutting off of his nose. There is no good beginning, but there will be a good end.

4. The fourth line, yang, shows its subject solitary amidst the prevailing disunion. But he meets with the good man represented by the first line, and they blend their sincere desires together. The position is one of peril, but there will be no mistake.

5. The fifth line, yin, shows that occasion for repentance will disappear. With his relative and minister he unites closely and readily as if he were biting through

a piece of skin. When he goes forward with this help, what error can there be?

6. The topmost line, yang, shows its subject solitary amidst the prevailing disunion. In the subject of the third line, he seems to see a pig bearing on its back a load of mud, or fancies there is a carriage full of ghosts. He first bends his bow against him and afterwards unbends it, for he discovers that he is not an assailant to injure, but a near relative. Going forward, he shall meet with genial rain, and there will be good fortune.

FROM THE WINGS:

In K'uei we have the symbol of Fire, which, when moved, tends upward, and that of a Marsh, whose waters, when moved, tend downward. We have also the symbols of two sisters living together, but whose wills do not move in the same direction.

We see how the inner trigram expressive of harmonious satisfaction is attached to the outer expressive of bright intelligence. These indications show that "in small matters there will still be good fortune."

Heaven and earth are separate and apart, but the work which they do is the same. Male and female are separate and apart, but with a common will they seek the same object. There is diversity between the myriad classes of beings, but there is an analogy between their several operations. Great indeed are the phenomena and the results of this condition of disunion and separation.

The trigram representing fire above, and that for the waters of a marsh below, form K'uei. The superior man, in accordance with this, where there is a general agreement, yet admits diversity.

1. "He meets with bad men and communicates with them": he does so to avoid the evil of their condemnation.

2. "He happens to meet with his lord in a byway": but he has not deviated for this meeting from the proper course.

3. "We see his carriage dragged back": this is indicated by the inappropriateness of the position of the line. "There is no good beginning, but there will be a good end": this arises from his meeting with the strong subject of the topmost line.

4. "They blend their sincere desires together, and there will be no error": their common aim is carried into effect.

5. "With his hereditary minister he unites closely and easily as if he were biting through a piece of skin": his going forward will afford ground for congratulation.

6. "The good fortune symbolized by meeting with genial rain" springs from the passing away of all doubts.

FROM THE NOTES OF JAMES LEGGE:

K'uei denotes disunion, a social state in which division and mutual alienation prevail, and the hexagram teaches how in small matters this condition may be healed, and the way prepared for the cure of the whole system.

K'AN, WATER
over
KEN, MOUNTAIN

39 CHIEN; DIFFICULTY

THE TEXT:

In the state indicated by Chien advantage will be found in the southwest, and the contrary in the northeast. It will be advantageous also to meet with the great man. In these circumstances, with firmness and correctness, there will be good fortune.

1. From the first line, yin, we learn that advance on the part of the subject will lead to greater difficulties, while remaining stationary will afford ground for praise.

2. The second line, yin, shows the minister of the king struggling with difficulty on difficulty, and not with a view to his own advantage.

3. The third line, yang, shows its subject advancing, but only to greater difficulties. He remains stationary and returns to his former associates.

4. The fourth line, yin, shows its subject advancing, but only to greater difficulties. He remains stationary and unites with the subject of the line above.

5. The fifth line, yang, shows its subject struggling with the greatest difficulties, while friends are coming to help him.

6. The topmost line, yin, shows its subject going forward, only to increase the difficulties, while his remaining stationary will be productive of great merit. There

will be good fortune, and it will be advantageous to meet with the great man.

Chien denotes difficulty. There is the trigram expressive of perilousness in front. When one, seeing the peril, can arrest his steps in accordance with the significance of the lower trigram, is he not wise?

The language of Chien, that "advantage will be found in the southwest," refers to the strong fifth line advanced and in the central place. That "there will be no advantage in the northeast" intimates that the way of dealing with the Chien state is exhausted. That "it will be advantageous to see the great man" intimates that advance will lead to achievement. That the places of the different lines after the first are those appropriate to them indicates firm correctness and good fortune, with which the regions of the kingdom are brought to their normal state. Great indeed is the work to be done in the time of Chien!

The trigram representing a mountain, and above it that for water, form Chien. The superior man, in accordance with this, turns round and examines himself, and cultivates his virtue.

1. "Advancing will conduct to greater difficulties, while remaining stationary will afford ground for praise": the proper course is to wait.

2. "The minister of the king struggles with difficulty on difficulty": in the end no blame will be attached to him.

3. "He advances, but only to greater difficulty; he remains stationary, and returns to his former associates": they, represented in the inner trigram, rejoice in him.

4. "To advance will only be to encounter greater difficulties; he remains stationary, and unites with the subject of the line above": that is in its proper place and has the solidity due to it in that position.

5. "He struggles with the greatest difficulties, while friends are coming to help him": he is in the central position, and possesses the requisite virtue.

6. "To advance will only increase the difficulties, while his remaining stationary will be productive of great merit": his aim is to assist the subject of the line inside of him.

"It will be advantageous to meet the great man": by his course he follows that noble lord of the figure.

FROM THE NOTES OF JAMES LEGGE:

Chien is the symbol for incompetency in the feet and legs, involving difficulty in walking; hence it is used in this hexagram to indicate a state of the kingdom which makes the government of it an arduous task. How this task may be successfully performed, now by activity on the part of the ruler, and now by a discreet inactivity: this is what the figure teaches, or at least gives hints about.

The T'uan seems to require three things—attention to place, the presence of the great man, and the firm observance of correctness—in order to cope successfully with the difficulties of the situation.

The upper or front trigram is K'an, the attribute of which is perilousness; the lower is Ken, of which the arresting, actively or passively, of movement or advance is the attribute. We can understand how the union of these attributes gives the ideas of difficulty and prudent caution.

CHEN, THUNDER
over
K'AN, WATER

40 CHIEH; RELIEF

THE TEXT:
In the state indicated by Chieh advantage will be found in the southwest. If no further operations be called for, there will be good fortune in coming back to the old conditions. If some operations be called for, there will be good fortune in the early conducting of them.

1. The first line, yin, shows that its subject will commit no error.

2. The second line, yang, shows its subject catch, in hunting, three foxes and obtain the yellow arrows. With firm correctness there will be good fortune.

3. The third line, yin, shows a porter with his burden, yet riding in a carriage. He will only tempt robbers to attack him. However firm and correct he may try to be, there will be cause for regret.

4. To the subject of the fourth line, yang, it is said, "Remove your toes. Friends will then come, between you and whom there will be mutual confidence."

5. The fifth line, yin, shows the superior man executing his function of removing whatever is injurious to the idea of the hexagram, in which case there will be good fortune, and confidence in him will be shown even by the small men.

6. In the sixth line, yin, we see a feudal prince with his bow shooting at a falcon on the top of a high wall, and hitting it. The effect of his action will be in every way advantageous.

FROM THE WINGS:

In Chieh we have the trigram expressive of peril going on to that expressive of movement. By movement there is an escape from the peril: this is the meaning of Chieh.

"In the state indicated by Chieh, advantage will be found in the southwest": the movement thus intimated will win all. That "there will be good fortune in coming back to the old conditions" shows that such action is that of the due medium. That "if some operations be necessary, there will be good fortune in the early conducting of them" shows that such operations will be successful.

When heaven and earth are freed from the grasp of winter, we have thunder and rain. When these come, the buds of the plants and trees that produce the various fruits begin to burst. Great indeed are the phenomena in the time indicated by Chieh.

The trigram representing thunder and that for rain, with these phenomena in a state of manifestation, form Chieh. The superior man, in accordance with this, forgives errors, and deals gently with crimes.

1. The fourth line, yang, and the first line, yin, here are in correlation: we judge rightly in saying that "its subject will commit no error."

2. "The good fortune springing from the firm correctness of the second line, yang," is due to its subject holding the due mean.

3. For "a porter with his burden to be riding in a carriage" is a thing to be ashamed of. "It is he himself that tempts the robbers to come."

4. "Remove your toes": the places of this line and of the third and first are all inappropriate to them.

5. When "the superior man executes his function of removing whatever is injurious to the idea of the hexagram," small men will of themselves retire.

6. "A prince with his bow shoots a falcon": thus he removes the promoters of rebellion.

FROM THE NOTES OF JAMES LEGGE:

Chieh is the symbol of loosing, untying a knot or unraveling a complication; and as the name of this hexagram, it denotes a condition in which the obstruction and difficulty indicated by the preceding Chien have been removed. The object of the author is to show, as if from the lines of the figure, how this new and better state of the kingdom is to be dealt with. See what is said on the T'uan of Chien for "the advantage to be found in the southwest." If further active operations be not necessary to complete the subjugation of the country, the sooner things fall into their old channels the better. The new masters of the kingdom should not be anxious to change all the old manners and ways. Let them do as the duke of Chou actually did do with the subjugated people of Shang. If further operations be necessary, let them be carried through without delay.

The subject becomes a hunter and disposes of unworthy men, represented by "the three foxes." He also gets the yellow arrows, the instruments used in war or in hunting, whose color is "correct," and whose form is "straight." His firm correctness will be good.

Line 3 is yin when it should be yang; and occupying,

as it does, the topmost place of the lower trigrams, it suggests the symbolism of a porter in a carriage. People will say, "How did he get there? The things cannot be his own." And robbers will attack and plunder him.

KEN, MOUNTAIN
over
TUI, MARSH

41   SUN; PAYMENT DUE

THE TEXT:

In what is denoted by Sun, if there be sincerity in
him who employs it, there will be great good fortune:
freedom from error; firmness and correctness that can
be maintained; and advantage in every movement that
shall be made. In what shall this sincerity in the exercise of Sun be employed? Even in sacrifice two baskets
of grain, though there be nothing else, may be presented.

1. The first line, yang, shows its subject suspending
his own affairs and hurrying away to help the subject
of the fourth line. He will commit no error, but let him
consider how far he should contribute of what is his
for the other.

2. The second line, yang, shows that it will be advantageous for its subject to maintain a firm correctness, and that action on his part will be evil. He can
give increase to his correlate without taking from himself.

3. The third line, yin, shows how of three men walking together, the number is diminished by one; and
how one, walking, finds his friend.

4. The fourth line, yin, shows its subject diminishing
the ailment under which he labors by making the sub-

ject of the first line hasten to help, and make him glad. There will be no error.

5. The fifth line, yin, shows parties adding to the stores of its subject ten pairs of tortoise shells, and accepting no refusal. There will be great good fortune.

6. The topmost line, yang, shows its subject giving increase to others without taking from himself. There will be no error. With firm correctness there will be good fortune. There will be advantage in every movement that shall be made. He will find ministers more than can be counted by their clans.

FROM THE WINGS

In Sun we see the lower trigram diminished and the upper added to. But the method of action implied in this operates also above or mounts upward also and operates.

In what shall this sincerity in the exercise of Sun be employed? "Even in sacrifice, two baskets of grain, though there be nothing else, may be presented": for these two baskets there ought to be the fitting time. There is a time when the strong should be diminished and the weak should be strengthened. Diminution and increase, overflowing and emptiness: these take place in harmony with the conditions of the time.

The trigram representing a mountain and beneath it that for the waters of a marsh form Sun. The superior man, in accordance with this, restrains his wrath and represses his desires.

1. "He suspends his own affairs and hurries away to help the subject of the fourth line": the subject of that upper line mingles his wishes with his.

2. "It will be advantageous for the subject of the

second line, yang, to maintain his firm correctness": his central position gives its character to his aim.

3. "One man, walking," finds his friend: when three are together, doubts rise among them.

4. "He diminishes the ailment under which he labors": this is matter for joy.

5. "The great good fortune attached to the fifth line, yin," is due to the blessing from above.

6. "He gives increase to others without taking from what is his own": he obtains his wish on a grand scale.

FROM THE NOTES OF JAMES LEGGE:

The interpretation of this hexagram is encompassed with great difficulties. Sun is the symbol for the idea of diminishing or diminution; and what is said has made it to be accepted as teaching the duty of the subject to take of what is his and contribute to his ruler, or the expenses of the government under which he lives; in other words, readily and cheerfully to pay his taxes. Possibly, king Wen may have seen in the figures the subject of taxation; but the symbolism of his son takes a much wider range. My own reading of the figure and Text comes near to the view of Cheng K'ang Ch'eng that "every diminution and repression of what we have in excess to bring it into accordance with right and reason is comprehended under Sun."

Let there be sincerity in doing this, and it will lead to the happiest results. The K'ang Hsi editors say: "What is meant by diminishing in this hexagram is the regulation of expenditure or contribution according to the time. This would vary in a family according to its poverty or wealth; and in a state according to the abundance or scantiness of its resources."

SUN, WIND
over
CHEN, THUNDER

42 I; Gifts Received

The Text:

I indicates that in the state which it denotes there will be advantage in every movement which shall be undertaken, that it will be advantageous even to cross the great stream.

1. The first line, yang, shows that it will be advantageous for its subject in his position to make a great movement. If it be greatly fortunate, no blame will be imputed to him.

2. The second line, yin, shows parties adding to the stores of its subject ten pairs of tortoise shells whose oracles cannot be opposed. Let him persevere in being firm and correct, and there will be good fortune. Let the king, having the virtues thus distinguished, employ them in presenting his offerings to God, and there will be good fortune.

3. The third line, yin, shows increase given to its subject by means of what is evil, so that he shall be led to good and be without blame. Let him be sincere and pursue the path of the Mean, so shall he secure the recognition of the ruler, like an officer who announces himself to his prince by the symbol of his rank.

4. The fourth line, yin, shows its subject pursuing the due course. His advice to his prince is followed.

He can with advantage be relied on in such a movement as that of removing the capital.

5. The fifth line, yang, shows its subject with sincere heart seeking to benefit all below. There need be no question about it; the result will be great good fortune. All below will with sincere heart acknowledge his goodness.

6. In the sixth line, yang, we see one to whose increase none will contribute, while many will seek to assail him. He observes no regular rule in the ordering of his heart. There will be evil.

FROM THE WINGS:

In I we see the upper trigram diminished and the lower added to. The satisfaction of the people in consequence of this is without limit. What descends from above reaches to all below, so great and brilliant is the course of its operation.

That "there will be advantage in every movement which shall be undertaken" appears from the central and correct positions of the second and fifth lines, and the general blessing the dispensing of which they imply.

That "it will be advantageous even to cross the great stream" appears from the action of wood shown in the figure.

I is made up of the trigrams expressive of movement and docility, through which there is daily advancement to an unlimited extent. We have also in it heaven dispensing and earth producing, leading to an increase without restriction of place. Everything in the method of this increase proceeds according to the requirements of the time.

The trigram representing wind and that for thunder form I. The superior man, in accordance with this, when he sees what is good moves toward it; and when he sees his errors he turns from them.

1. "If the movement be greatly fortunate, no blame will be imputed to him": though it is not for one in so low a position to have to do with great affairs.

2. "Parties add to his stores": they come from beyond his immediate circle to do so.

3. "Increase is given by means of what is evil and difficult": as he has in himself the qualities called forth.

4. "His advice to his prince is followed": his only object in it being the increase of the general good.

5. "The ruler with sincere heart seeks to benefit all below": there need be no question about the result. "All below with sincere heart acknowledge his goodness": he gets what he desires on a great scale.

6. "To his increase none will contribute": this expresses but half the result. "Many will seek to assail him": they will come from beyond his immediate circle to do so.

FROM THE NOTES OF JAMES LEGGE:

I has the opposite meaning to Sun and is the symbol of addition or increasing. What king Wen had in his mind, in connection with the hexagram, was a ruler or a government operating so as to dispense benefits to and increase the resources of all the people.

The mention of "the action of wood" has reference to Sun, which is the symbol of both wind and wood. From wood boats and ships are made, on which the great stream may be crossed.

I spoils the high, gives to the low;
The people feel intense delight.
Down from above to all below,

The blessing goes, so large and bright.
Success will every movement mark,
Central its source, its course aright.
The great stream even may be crossed,
When planks of wood their strength unite.
I movement shows and docile feet,
Which progress day by day invite.
Heaven gives; productive earth responds;
Increase crowns every vale and height;
And ceaselessly it hastens on,
Each season's gifts quick to requite.

TUI, MARSH
over
CH'IEN, HEAVEN

43 KUAI; REMOVAL

THE TEXT:

Kuai requires the exhibition of the culprit's guilt in
the royal court, and a sincere and earnest appeal for
sympathy and support, with a consciousness of the
peril involved in cutting off the criminal. He should
also make announcement in his own city, and show that
it will not be well to have recourse at once to arms.
In this way there will be advantage in whatever he
shall go forward to.

1. The first line, yang, shows its subject in the pride
of strength advancing with his toes. He goes forward
but will not succeed. There will be ground for blame.

2. The second line, yang, shows its subject full of
apprehension and appealing for sympathy and help.
Late at night hostile measures may be taken against
him, but he need not be anxious about them.

3. The third line, yang, shows its subject about to
advance with strong and determined looks. There will
be evil. But the superior man, bent on cutting off the
criminal, will walk alone and encounter the rain, till he
be hated by his proper associates as if he were con-
taminated by the others. In the end there will be no
blame against him.

4. The fourth line, yang, shows one from whose buttocks the skin has been stripped, and who walks slowly

and with difficulty. If he could act like a sheep led after its companions, occasion for repentance would disappear. But though he hear these words, he will not believe them.

5. The fifth line, yang, shows the small men like a bed of purslain, which ought to be uprooted with the utmost determination. The subject of the line having such determination, his action, in harmony with his central position, will lead to no error or blame.

6. The sixth line, yin, shows its subject without any helpers on whom to call. His end will be evil.

From the Wings:

Kuai is the symbol of displacing or removing. We see in the figure the yang lines displacing the yin. We have in it the attributes of strength and complacency. There is displacement, but harmony continues.

"The exhibition of the criminal's guilt in the royal courtyard" is suggested by the one yin line mounted on the five yang lines.

There "is an earnest and sincere appeal for sympathy and support, and a consciousness of the peril involved in the undertaking": it is the realization of this danger which makes the method of compassing the object brilliant.

"He should make an announcement in his own city, and show that it will not be well to have recourse at once to arms": if he have recourse to arms, what he prefers will soon be exhausted.

"There will be advantage in whatever he shall go forward to": when the growth of the strong lines has been completed, there will be an end of the displacement.

The trigram representing heaven and that for the waters of a marsh mounting above it form Kuai. The superior man, in accordance with this, bestows emolument on those below him and dislikes allowing his gifts to accumulate undispensed.

1. "Without being able to succeed, he goes forward": this is an error.

2. "Though hostile measures be taken against him, he need not be anxious": he pursues the course of the due mean.

3. "The superior man looks bent on cutting off the culprit": there will in the end be no error.

4. "He walks slowly and with difficulty": he is not in the place appropriate to him. "He hears these words but does not believe them": he hears but does not understand.

5. "If his action be in harmony with his central position, there will be no error": but his standing in the due mean is not yet clearly displayed.

6. "There is the misery of having none on whom to call": the end will be that he cannot continue any longer.

FROM THE NOTES OF JAMES LEGGE:

In Kuai we have the hexagram of the third month, when the last remnant, cold and dark, of winter, represented by the sixth line, is about to disappear before the advance of the warm and bright days of the approaching summer. In the yin line at the top king Wen saw the symbol of a small or bad man, a feudal prince or high minister, lending his power to maintain a corrupt government, or a dynasty that was waxen old and ready to vanish away. In the five yang lines he saw the representatives of good order or, it might be, the dynasty which was to supersede the other. This then is the subject of the hexagram, how bad men, statesmen corrupt and yet powerful, are to be put out of the way. And he who would accomplish the task must do so by the force of his character more than by force of arms, and by producing a general sympathy on his side.

The T'uan says that he must openly denounce the criminal in the court, seek to awaken general sympathy, and at the same time go about his enterprise, conscious of its difficulty and danger. Among his own adherents he must make it understood how unwillingly he takes up arms. Then let him go forward, and success will attend him.

We have the symbol of a culprit, who, according to the ancient and modern custom of Chinese courts, has been bastinadoed till he presents the appearance in the Text. Alone he can do nothing; if he could follow others, like a sheep led along, he might accomplish something, but he will not listen to advice.

Purslain grows in shady places, and hence we find it here in close contiguity to the topmost line, which is yin.

44 KOU; ENCOUNTER

THE TEXT:

Kou shows a female who is bold and strong. It will not be good to marry such a female.

1. The first line, yin, shows how its subject should be kept like a carriage tied and fastened to a metal drag, in which case with firm correctness there will be good fortune. But if he move in any direction, evil will appear. He will be like a lean pig, which is sure to keep jumping about.

2. The second line, yang, shows its subject with a wallet of fish. There will be no error. But it will not be well to let the subject of the first line go forward to the guests.

3. The third line, yang, shows one from whose buttocks the skin has been stripped so that he walks with difficulty. The position is perilous, but there will be no great error.

4. The fourth line, yang, shows its subject with his wallet, but no fish in it. This will give rise to evil.

5. The fifth line, yang, shows its subject as a medlar tree overspreading the gourd beneath it. If he keeps his brilliant qualities concealed, a good issue will descend as from Heaven.

6. The sixth line, yang, shows its subject receiving

others on his horns. There will be occasion for regret, but there will be no error.

FROM THE WINGS:

Kou has the significance of unexpectedly coming on. We see in it the yin line coming unexpectedly on the yang ones.

"It will not be good to marry such a female": one so symbolized should not be long associated with.

Heaven and earth meeting together as here represented, all the variety of natural things become fully displayed.

When a yang line finds itself in the central and correct position, good government will greatly prevail all under the sky.

Great indeed is the significance of what has to be done at the time indicated by Kou!

The trigram representing wind and that for the sky above it form Kou. The sovereign, in accordance with this, delivers his charges, and promulgates his announcements throughout the four quarters of the kingdom.

1. "Tied and fastened to a metal drag": this describes the arrest of the yin line in its advancing course.

2. "He has a wallet of fish": it is right for him not to allow the subject of the first line to get to the guests.

3. "He walks with difficulty": but his steps have not yet been drawn into the course of the first line.

4. "The evil" indicated by there being "no fish in the wallet" is owing to the subject of the line keeping himself aloof from the people.

5. "The subject of the fifth line, yang, keeps his brilliant qualities concealed": as is indicated by his central and correct position.

"The good issue descends as from Heaven": his aim does not neglect the ordinances of Heaven.

6. "He receives others on his horns": he is exhausted at his greatest height, and there will be cause for regret.

FROM THE NOTES OF JAMES LEGGE:

In the first line, yin, Wen saw the symbol of the small or unworthy man, beginning to insinuate himself into the government of the country.

Kou is defined as giving the idea of suddenly and casually encountering or meeting with.

TUI, MARSH
over
K'UN, EARTH

45 Ts'ui; Gatherings

THE TEXT:

In the state denoted by Ts'ui the king will repair to his ancestral temple. It will be advantageous also to meet with the great man; and then there will be progress and success, though the advantage must come through firm correctness. The use of great victims will conduce to good fortune; and in whatever direction movement is made, it will be advantageous.

1. The first line, yin, shows its subject with a sincere desire for union but unable to carry it out, so that disorder is brought into the sphere of his union. If he cry out for help to his proper correlate, all at once his tears will give place to smiles. He need not mind the temporary difficulty; as he goes forward, there will be no error.

2. The second line, yin, shows its subject led forward by his correlate. There will be good fortune and freedom from error. There is entire sincerity, and in that case even the small offerings of the vernal sacrifices are acceptable.

3. The third line, yin, shows its subject striving after union and seeming to sigh, yet nowhere finding any advantage. If he go forward, he will not err, though there may be some small cause for regret.

4. The fourth line, yang, shows its subject in such a state that, if he be greatly fortunate, he will receive no blame.

5. The fifth line, yang, shows the union of all under its subject in the place of dignity. There will be no error. If any do not have confidence in him, let him see to it that his virtue be great, long-continued, and firmly correct, and all occasion for repentance will disappear.

6. The topmost line, yin, shows its subject sighing and weeping; but there will be no error.

FROM THE WINGS:

Ts'ui indicates the condition of union or being collected. We have in it the symbol of docile obedience going on to satisfaction. There is the yang line in the central place, and rightly responded to. Hence comes the idea of union.

"The king will repair to his ancestral temple": with the utmost filial piety he presents his offerings to the spirits of his ancestors.

"It will be advantageous to meet the great man, and there will then be prosperity and success": the union effected by him will be on and through what is correct.

"The use of great victims will conduce to good fortune; and in whatsoever direction movement is made, it will be advantageous": all is done in accordance with the ordinances of Heaven.

When we look at the way in which the gatherings here shown take place, the natural tendencies in the outward action of heaven and earth and of all things can be seen.

The trigram representing the earth and that for the waters of a marsh raised above it form Ts'ui. The superior man, in accordance with this, has his weapons of war put in good repair, to be prepared against unforeseen contingencies.

1. "In consequence disorder is brought into the sphere of his union": his mind and aim are thrown into confusion.

2. "He is led forward; there will be good fortune and freedom from error": the virtue proper to his central place has not undergone any change.

3. "If he go forward, he will not err": in the subject of the topmost line there is humility and condescension.

4. "If he be grandly fortunate, he will receive no blame": this condition is necessary, because his position is not the one proper to him.

5. "There is the union of all under him in the place of dignity": but his mind and aim have not yet been brilliantly displayed.

6. "He sighs and weeps": he does not yet rest in his topmost position.

FROM THE NOTES OF JAMES LEGGE:

Ts'ui denotes collecting together, or things so collected.

K'UN, EARTH
over
SUN, WIND

46 SHENG; ADVANCE

THE TEXT:

Sheng indicates that under its conditions there will be great progress and success. Seeking by the qualities implied in it to meet with the great man, its subject need have no anxiety. Advance to the south will be fortunate.

1. The first line, yin, shows its subject advancing upward with the welcome of those above him. There will be great good fortune.

2. The second line, yang, shows its subject with that sincerity which will make even the small offerings of the vernal sacrifice acceptable. There will be no error.

3. The third line, yang, shows its subject ascending upward as into an empty city.

4. The fourth line, yin, shows its subject employed by the king to present his offerings on mount Chi. There will be good fortune; there will be no mistake.

5. The fifth line, yin, shows its subject firmly correct and therefore enjoying good fortune. He ascends the stairs with all due ceremony.

6. The sixth line, yin, shows its subject advancing upward blindly. Advantage will be found in a ceaseless maintenance of firm correctness.

FROM THE WINGS:

We find the yin line, as it finds the opportunity, ascending upward.

We have the attribute of flexibility and that of obedience; we have the yang line below and its proper correlate above: these things indicate that there will be "great progress and success."

"Seeking by the qualities implied in Sheng to meet with the great man, its subject need have no anxiety": there will be ground for congratulation.

"Advance to the south will be fortunate": his aim will be carried out.

The trigram representing wood and that for the earth with the wood growing in the midst of it form Sheng. The superior man, in accordance with this, pays careful attention to his virtue, and accumulates the small developments of it till it is high and great.

1. "He is welcomed in his advance upward, and there will be great good fortune": the subjects of the upper trigram are of the same mind with him.

2. "The sincerity of the subject of the second line, yang," affords occasion for joy.

3. "He advances upward as into an empty city": he has no doubt or hesitation.

4. "The king employs him to present his offerings on mount Chi": such a service of spiritual beings is according to their mind.

5. "He is firmly correct and will therefore enjoy good fortune. He ascends the stairs with all due ceremony": he grandly succeeds in his aim.

6. "He blindly advances upward" and is in the highest place: but there is decay in store for him, and he will not preserve his riches.

FROM THE NOTES OF JAMES LEGGE:

The character Sheng is used of advancing in an upward direction, "advancing and ascending."

TUI, MARSH
over
K'AN, WATER

47   K'un; Restrictions

The Text:

In the condition denoted by K'un there may yet be progress and success. For the firm and correct, the really great man, there will be good fortune. He will fall into no error. If he make speeches, his words cannot be made good.

1. The first line, yin, shows its subject with bare buttocks straitened under the stump of a tree. He enters a dark valley and for three years has no prospect of deliverance.

2. The second line, yang, shows its subject straitened amidst his wine and viands. There come to him anon the red knee-covers of the ruler. It will be well for him to maintain his sincerity as in sacrificing. Active operations on his part will lead to evil, but he will be free from blame.

3. The third line, yin, shows its subject straitened before a frowning rock. He lays hold of thorns. He enters his palace and does not see his wife. There will be evil.

4. The fourth line, yang, shows its subject proceeding very slowly to help the subject of the first line, who is straitened by the carriage adorned with metal in front of him. There will be occasion for regret, but the end will be good.

5. The fifth line, yang, shows its subject with his nose and feet cut off. He is straitened by his ministers in their scarlet aprons. He is leisurely in his movements, however, and is satisfied. It will be well for him to be as sincere as in sacrificing to spiritual beings.

6. The sixth line, yin, shows its subject straitened, as if bound with creepers; or in a high and dangerous position, and saying to himself, "If I move, I shall repent it." If he do repent of former errors, there will be good fortune in his going forward.

FROM THE WINGS:

In K'un we see the yang lines covered and obscured by the yin.

We have in it the attributes of perilousness going on to that of satisfaction. Who is it but the superior man that, though straitened, still does not fail in making progress to his proper end?

"For the firm and correct, the really great man, there will be good fortune": this is shown by the central positions of the yang lines.

"If he make speeches, his words cannot be made good": to be fond of arguing or pleading is the way to be reduced to extremity.

The trigram representing a marsh, and below it that for a defile, which has drained the other dry so that there is no water in it, form K'un. The superior man, in accordance with this, will sacrifice his life in order to carry out his purpose.

1. "He enters a dark valley": so benighted is he, and without clear vision.

2. "He is straitened amidst his wine and viands": but his position is central, and there will be ground for congratulation.

3. "He lays hold of thorns": this is suggested by the position of the yin above the yang line.

"He enters his palace and does not see his wife": this is inauspicious.

4. "He proceeds very slowly to help the subject of the first line": his aim is directed to help that lower line. Although he is not in his appropriate place, he and that other will in the end be together.

5. "His nose and feet are cut off": his aim has not yet been gained.

"He is leisurely, however, in his movements and is satisfied": his position is central and his virtue is correct.

"It will be well for him to be as sincere as in sacrificing": so shall he receive blessing.

6. "He is straitened as if bound with creepers": his spirit and action are unsuitable.

"He says, 'If I move, I shall repent of it.' And he does repent of former errors, which leads to good fortune": so he now goes on.

FROM THE NOTES OF JAMES LEGGE:

The character K'un presents us with the picture of a tree within an enclosure, "a tree," according to Tai Tung, "not allowed to spread its branches." However this be, the term conveys the idea of being straitened and distressed. This hexagram indicates a state of things in which the order and government that would conduce to the well-being of the country can hardly get the development, which, by skillful management on the part of "the great man" and others, is finally secured for them.

K'AN, WATER
over
SUN, WIND

48 CHING; WELLS

THE TEXT:

Looking at Ching we think of how the site of a town may be changed, while the fashion of its wells undergoes no change. The water of a well never disappears and never receives any great increase, and those who come and those who go can draw and enjoy the benefit. If the drawing have nearly been accomplished, but, before the rope has quite reached the water, the bucket is broken, this is evil.

1. The first line, yin, shows a well so muddy that men will not drink of it; or an old well to which neither birds nor other creatures resort.

2. The second line, yang, shows a well from which by a hole the water escapes and flows away to the shrimps and such small creatures among the grass, or one the water of which leaks away from a broken basket.

3. The third line, yang, shows a well, which has been cleared out, but is not used. Our hearts are sorry for this, for the water might be drawn out and used. If the king were only intelligent, both he and we might receive the benefit of it.

4. The fourth line, yin, shows a well, the lining of which is well laid. There will be no error.

5. The fifth line, yang, shows a clear, limpid well, the waters from whose cold springs are freely drunk.

6. The topmost line, yin, shows the water from the well brought to the top, which is not allowed to be covered. This suggests the idea of sincerity. There will be great good fortune.

FROM THE WINGS:

We have the symbol of wood in the water and the raising of the water; which gives us the idea of a well. A well supplies nourishment and is not itself exhausted.

"The site of a town may be changed, while the fashion of its wells undergoes no change": this is indicated by the yang lines in the second and fifth places.

"The drawing is nearly accomplished, but the rope has not yet reached the water of the well": its service has not yet been accomplished.

"The bucket is broken": it is this that occasions evil.

The trigram representing wood and above it that for water form Ching. The superior man, in accordance with this, comforts the people, and stimulates them to mutual helpfulness.

1. "A well so muddy that men will not drink of it": this is indicated by the low position of the line.

"An old well to which the birds do not come": it has been forsaken in the course of time.

2. "A well from which by a hole the water escapes, and flows away to the shrimps": the subject of this second line has none cooperating with him above.

3. "The well has been cleared out, but is not used": even passersby would be sorry for this.

A prayer is made "that the king were intelligent": for then blessing would be received.

4. "A well the lining of which is well laid. There will be no error": the well has been put in good repair.

5. "The waters from the cold spring are freely drunk": this is indicated by the central and correct position of the line.

6. "The great good fortune" at the topmost place indicates the grand accomplishment of the idea in the hexagram.

FROM THE NOTES OF JAMES LEGGE:

Ching, which gives its name to this hexagram, is the symbol of a well.

TUI, MARSH
over
LI, FIRE

49   Ko; Change

THE TEXT:

What takes place as indicated by Ko is believed in only after it has been accomplished. There will be great progress and success. Advantage will come from being firm and correct. In that case occasion for repentance will disappear.

1. The first line, yang, shows its subject as if bound with the skin of a yellow ox.

2. The second line, yin, shows its subject making his changes after some time has passed. Action taken will be fortunate. There will be no error.

3. The third line, yang, shows that action taken by its subject will be evil. Though he be firm and correct, his position is perilous. If the change he contemplates have been three times fully discussed, he will be believed in.

4. The fourth line, yang, shows occasion for repentance disappearing. Let him be believed in; and though he change existing ordinances, there will be good fortune.

5. The fifth line, yang, shows the great man producing his changes as the tiger changes his stripes. Before he divines and proceeds to action, faith has been reposed in him.

6. The sixth line, yin, shows the superior man producing his changes as the leopard changes his spots, while small men change their faces and show their obedience. To go forward now would lead to evil, but there will be good fortune in abiding firm and correct.

FROM THE WINGS:

In Ko we see water and fire extinguishing each other; we see also two daughters dwelling together, but with their minds directed to different objects: on account of these things it is called the hexagram of Change.

"It is believed in only after it has been accomplished": when the change has been made, faith is accorded to it.

We have cultivated intelligence as the basis of pleased satisfaction, suggesting "great progress and success," coming from what is correct.

When change thus takes place in the proper way, "occasion for repentance disappears."

Heaven and earth undergo their changes, and the four seasons complete their functions. T'ang changed the appointment of the line of Hsia to the throne, and Wu that of the line of Shang, in accordance with the will of Heaven and in response to the wishes of men. Great indeed is what takes place in a time of change.

The trigram representing the waters of a marsh and that for fire in the midst of them form Ko. The superior man, in accordance with this, regulates his astronomical calculations and makes clear the seasons and times.

1. "He is bound with the skin of a yellow ox": he should in his circumstances be taking action.

2. "He makes his changes when some time has passed": what he does will be matter of admiration.

3. "The change contemplated has been three times fully discussed": to what else should attention now be directed?

4. "The good fortune consequent on changing existing ordinances" is due to the faith reposed in his aims.

5. "The great man produces his changes as the tiger does when he changes his stripes": their beauty becomes more brilliant.

6. "The superior man produces his changes as the leopard does when he changes his spots": their beauty becomes more elegant.

"Small men change their faces": they show themselves prepared to follow their ruler.

FROM THE NOTES OF JAMES LEGGE:

The character called Ko is used here in the sense of changing.

It is assumed in the T'uan that change is viewed by people generally with suspicion and dislike, and should not be made hastily. When made as a necessity, and its good effects appear, the issues will be great and good. A proved necessity for them beforehand; and a firm correctness in the conduct of them: these are the conditions by which changes should be regulated.

50 TING; CAULDRON

THE TEXT:

Ting gives the intimation of great progress and success.

1. The first line, yin, shows the cauldron overthrown and its feet turned up. But there will be advantage in its getting rid of what was bad in it. Or it shows us the concubine whose position is improved by means of her son. There will be no error.

2. The second line, yang, shows the cauldron with the things to be cooked in it. If its subject can say, "My enemy dislikes me, but he cannot approach me," there will be good fortune.

3. The third line, yang, shows the cauldron with the places of its ears changed. The progress of its subject is thus stopped. The fat flesh of the pheasant which is in the cauldron will not be eaten. But the genial rain will come, and the grounds for repentance will disappear. There will be good fortune in the end.

4. The fourth line, yang, shows the cauldron with its feet broken, and its contents, designed for the ruler's use, overturned and spilled. Its subject will be made to blush for shame. There will be evil.

5. The fifth line, yin, shows the cauldron with yellow ears and rings of metal in them. There will be advantage through being firm and correct.

6. The sixth line, yang, shows the cauldron with rings of jade. There will be great good fortune, and all action taken will be in every way advantageous.

FROM THE WINGS:

In Ting we have symbolically the figure of a cauldron. We see the symbol of wood entering into that of fire, which suggests the idea of cooking. The sages cooked their offerings in order to present them to God, and made great feasts to nourish their wise and able ministers.

We have the symbol of flexible obedience, and that which denotes ears quick of hearing and eyes clearsighted. We have also the yin line advanced and acting above, in the central place, and responded to by the yang line below. All these things give the idea of "great progress and success."

The trigram representing wood and above it that for fire form Ting. The superior man, in accordance with this, keeps his every position correct, and maintains secure the appointment of Heaven.

1. "The cauldron is overturned, and its feet turned upward": but this is not all contrary to what is right.

2. "There is the cauldron with the things to be cooked in it": let the subject of the line be careful where he goes.

"My enemy dislikes me": but there will in the end be no fault to which he can point.

3. "There is the cauldron with the places for its ears changed": its subject has failed in what was required of him in his situation.

4. "The contents designed for the ruler's use are overturned and spilled": how can the subject of the line be trusted?

5. "The cauldron has yellow ears": the central position of the line is taken as a proof of the solid virtue of its subject.

6. "The rings of jade" are at the very top: the strong and the weak meet in their due proportions.

FROM THE NOTES OF JAMES LEGGE:

Ting was originally a pictorial character, representing a cauldron with three feet and two ears, used for cooking and preparing food for the table and the altar. The picture has disappeared from the character, but it is said that in the hexagram we have an outline from which fancy may construct the vessel.

The lower line, divided, represents its feet; lines 2, 3, 4, all undivided, represent the body of it; line 5, divided, represents its two ears; and line 6, undivided, the handle by which it was carried, or suspended from a hook.

Ting and Ching (48) are the only two hexagrams named from things in ordinary use with men; and they are both descriptive of the government's work of nourishing.

In the cauldron is good fare,
See my foe with angry glare;
But touch me he does not dare.

CHEN, THUNDER
Repeated

51 CHEN; MOVING FORWARD

THE TEXT:

Chen gives the intimation of ease and development. When the time of movement which it indicates comes, the subject of the hexagram will be found looking out with apprehension, and yet smiling and talking cheerfully. When the movement like a crash of thunder terrifies all within a hundred li, he will be like the sincere worshiper who is not startled into letting go his ladle and cup of sacrificial spirits.

1. The first line, yang, shows its subject looking out with apprehension and afterward smiling and talking cheerfully. There will be good fortune.

2. The second line, yin, shows its subject, when the movement approaches, in a position of peril. He judges it better to let go the articles in his possession, and to ascend a very lofty height. There is no occasion for him to pursue after the things he has let go; in seven days he will find them.

3. The third line, yin, shows its subject distraught amid the startling movements going on. If those movements excite him to right action, there will be no mistake.

4. The fourth line, yang, shows its subject, amid the startling movements, supinely sinking deeper in the mud.

5. The fifth line, yin, shows its subject going and coming amidst the startling movements of the time, and always in peril; perhaps he will not incur loss, but find business which he can accomplish.

6. The topmost line, yin, shows its subject amidst the startling movements of the time, in breathless dismay and looking round him with trembling apprehension. If he take action, there will be evil. If, while the startling movements have not reached his own person and his neighborhood, he were to take precautions, there would be no error, though his relatives might still speak against him.

FROM THE WINGS:

Chen gives the intimation of ease and development.

"When the time of movement which it indicates comes, its subject will be found looking out with apprehension": that feeling of dread leads to happiness. "And yet smiling and talking cheerfully": the issue of his dread is that he adopts proper laws for his course.

"The movement like a crash of thunder terrifies all within a hundred li": it startles the distant and frightens the near.

"He will be like the sincere worshiper, who is not startled into letting go his ladle and cup of sacrificial spirits": he makes his appearance, and maintains his ancestral temple and the altars of the spirits of the land and grain, as presiding at all sacrifices.

The trigram representing thunder, being repeated, forms Chen. The superior man, in accordance with this, is fearful and apprehensive, cultivates his virtue, and examines his faults.

1. "When the time of movement comes, he will be

found looking out with apprehension": that feeling of dread leads to happiness.

"He yet smiles and talks cheerfully": the issue of his dread is that he adopts proper laws for his course.

2. "When the movement approaches, he is in a position of peril": a yin line is mounted on a yang.

3. "He is distraught amid the startling movements going on": the third line is in a position unsuitable to it.

4. "Amid the startling movements, he sinks supinely in the mud": the light in him has not yet been brilliantly developed.

5. "He goes and comes amid the startling movements, and always in peril": full of risk are his doings.

"What he has to do has to be done in his central position": far will he be from incurring any loss.

6. "Amid the startling movements he is in breathless dismay": he has not found out the course of the due mean.

"Though evil threatens, he will not fall into error": he is afraid of being warned by his neighbors.

FROM THE NOTES OF JAMES LEGGE:

The hexagram may be taken as representing the crash or peal of thunder; but we have seen that the attribute or virtue of the trigram is "moving, exciting power." Symbolically, the character is indicative of movement taking place in society or in the kingdom.

52 KEN; STOPPING, RESTING

THE TEXT:

When one's resting is like that of the back, and he loses all consciousness of self; when he walks in his courtyard and does not see any of the persons in it, there will be no error.

1. The first line, yin, shows its subject keeping his toes at rest. There will be no error; but it will be advantageous for him to be persistently firm and correct.

2. The second line, yin, shows its subject keeping the calves of his legs at rest. He cannot help the subject of the line above whom he follows, and is dissatisfied in his mind.

3. The third line, yang, shows its subject keeping his loins at rest, and separating the ribs from the body below. The situation is perilous, and the heart glows with suppressed excitement.

4. The fourth line, yin, shows its subject keeping his trunk at rest. There will be no error.

5. The fifth line, yin, shows its subject keeping his jawbones at rest, so that his words are all orderly. Occasion for repentance will disappear.

6. The sixth line, yang, shows its subject devotedly maintaining his restfulness. There will be good fortune.

FROM THE WINGS:

Ken denotes stopping or resting; resting when it is

the time to rest, and acting when it is the time to act. When one's movements and restings all take place at the proper time, his way is brilliant and intelligent.

Resting on one's resting-point is resting in one's proper place. The upper and lower lines of the hexagram exactly correspond to each other, but are without any interaction; hence it is said that "the subject of the hexagram has no consciousness of self; that when he walks in his courtyard, he does not see any of the persons in it, and that there will be no error."

Two trigrams representing a mountain, one over the other, form Ken. The superior man, in accordance with this, does not go in his thoughts beyond the duties of the position in which he is.

1. "He keeps his toes at rest": he does not fail in what is correct.

2. "He cannot help him whom he follows": he whom he follows will not retreat to listen to him.

3. "He keeps the loins at rest": the danger from his doing so produces a glowing heat in the heart.

4. "He keeps the trunk of his body at rest": he keeps himself free from agitation.

5. "He keeps his cheek bones at rest": in harmony with his central position he acts correctly.

6. "There is good fortune through his devotedly maintaining his restfulness": to the end he shows himself generous and good.

FROM THE NOTES OF JAMES LEGGE:

The trigram Ken represents a mountain. Mountains rise up grandly from the surface of the earth, and their masses rest on it in quiet and solemn majesty; and they serve also to arrest the onward progress of the traveler.

Hence the attribute ascribed to Ken is twofold; it is both active and passive, resting and arresting. The character is used in this hexagram with both of those significations. As the name of the figure, it denotes the mental characteristic of resting in what is right; especially resting, as it is expressed by Chinese critics, "in principle," that which is right, on the widest scale, and in the absolute conception of the mind; and that which is right in every different position in which a man can be placed. This is the theme of the hexagram. The symbolism is taken from different parts of the body as in Hexagram 31.

In society, he who realizes the idea of the hexagram is still alone, and does not allow himself to be distracted from the contemplation and following of principle. He is not a recluse, however; his distinction is that he maintains a supreme regard to principle—when alone and when mingling with others.

SUN, WIND
over
KEN, MOUNTAIN

53 CHIEN; GRADUAL PROGRESS

THE TEXT:

Chien suggests to us the marriage of a young lady and the good fortune attending it. There will be advantage in being firm and correct.

1. The first line, yin, shows the wild geese gradually approaching the shore. A young officer in similar circumstances will be in a position of danger, and be spoken against; but there will be no error.

2. The second line, yin, shows the geese gradually approaching the large rocks, where they eat and drink joyfully and at ease. There will be good fortune.

3. The third line, yang, shows them gradually advanced to the dry plains. It suggests also the idea of a husband who goes on an expedition from which he does not return, and of a wife who is pregnant, but will not nourish her child. There will be evil. The case symbolized might be advantageous in resisting plunderers.

4. The fourth line, yin, shows the geese gradually advanced to the trees. They may light on the flat branches. There will be no error.

5. The fifth line, yang, shows the geese gradually advanced to the high mound. It suggests the idea of a wife who for three years does not become pregnant;

but in the end the natural issue cannot be prevented. There will be good fortune.

6. The sixth line, yang, shows the geese gradually advanced to the heights beyond. Their feathers can be used as ornaments. There will be good fortune.

FROM THE WINGS:

The advance indicated by Chien is like the marrying of a young lady which is attended by good fortune.

The lines as they advance get into their correct places: this indicates the achievements of a successful progress.

The advance is made according to correctness: the subject of the hexagram might rectify his country.

Among the places of the hexagram we see the strong undivided line in the center.

"In the attributes of restfulness and flexible penetration we have the assurance of an onward movement that is inexhaustible.

The trigram representing a mountain and above it that for a tree form Chien. The superior man, in accordance with this, attains to and maintains his extraordinary virtue, and makes the manners of the people good.

1. "The danger of a small officer as represented in the first line" is owing to no fault of his in the matter of what is right.

2. "They eat and drink joyfully and at ease": but not without having earned their food.

3. "A husband goes and does not return": he separates himself from his comrades.

"A wife is pregnant, but will not nourish her child": she has failed in her proper course.

"It might be advantageous in resisting plunderers": by acting as here indicated men would preserve one another.

4. "They may light on the flat branches": there is docility in the line going on to flexible penetration.

5. "In the end the natural issue cannot be prevented. There will be good fortune": the subject of the line will get what he desires.

6. "Their feathers can be used as ornaments. There will be good fortune": the object and character of the subject of the line cannot be disturbed.

FROM THE NOTES OF JAMES LEGGE:

Chien is ordinarily used in the sense of gradually; but there is connected with that the idea also of progress or advance. The element of meaning in the character is the symbol of water; and the whole of it denotes gradual advance, like the soaking in of water.

The goose from the most ancient times played an important part in the marriage ceremonies of the Chinese; and this may have suggested the use of it in the symbolism of the different lines. Its habits as a bird of passage, and flying in processional order, admirably suited the writer's purpose.

CHEN, THUNDER
over
TUI, MARSH

54   KUEI MEI; GOING HOME

THE TEXT:

Kuei Mei indicates that under the conditions which it denotes action will be evil, and in no wise advantageous.

1. The first line, yang, shows the younger sister married off in a position ancillary to the real wife. It suggests the idea of a person lame on one leg who yet manages to tramp along. Going forward will be fortunate.

2. The second line, yang, shows her blind of one eye, and yet able to see. There will be advantage in her maintaining the firm correctness of a solitary widow.

3. The third line, yin, shows the younger sister who was to be married off in a mean position. She returns and accepts an ancillary position.

4. The fourth line, yang, shows the younger sister who is to be married off protracting the time. She may be late in being married, but the time will come.

5. The fifth line, yin, reminds us of the marrying of the younger sister of king Ti-yi. The sleeves of the princess were not equal to those of the younger sister, who accompanied her in an inferior capacity. The case suggests the thought of the moon almost full. There will be good fortune.

6. The sixth line, yin, shows the young lady bearing the basket, but without anything in it, and the gentleman slaughtering the sheep, but without blood flowing from it. There will be no advantage in any way.

From the Wings:

By Kuei Mei, the marrying away of a younger sister, the great and righteous relation between heaven and earth is suggested to us. If heaven and earth were to have no intercommunication, things would not grow and flourish as they do. The marriage of a younger sister is the end of her maidenhood and the beginning of her motherhood.

We have in the hexagram the desire of pleasure and, on the ground of that, movement following. The marrying away is of a younger sister.

"Any action will be evil": the places of the lines are not those appropriate to them.

The trigram representing the waters of a marsh and over it that for thunder form Kuei Mei. The superior man, in accordance with this, having regard to the far-distant end, knows the mischief that may be done at the beginning.

1. "The younger sister is married off in a position ancillary to that of the real wife": it is the constant practice for such a case.

"Lame on one leg, she is able to tramp along": she can render helpful service.

2. "There will be advantage in maintaining the firm correctness of a solitary widow": the subject of the line has not changed from the constancy proper to a wife.

3. "The younger sister who was to be married off is in a mean position": this is shown by the improprieties indicated in the line.

4. The purpose in "protracting the time" is that, after waiting, the thing may be done all the better.

5. "The sleeves of the younger sister of king Ti-yi, when she was married away, were not equal to those of her half-sister, who accompanied her": such was her noble character, indicated by the central position of the line.

6. "What is said in the sixth line about there being nothing in the basket" shows that the subject of it is carrying an empty basket.

FROM THE NOTES OF JAMES LEGGE:

Mei Kuei is a common way of saying that a young lady is married, or, literally, "is going home."

A feudal prince was said to marry nine ladies at once. The principal of them was the bride who was to be the proper wife, and she was attended by two others, virgins from her father's harem; a cousin, and a half-sister, a daughter of her father by another mother of inferior rank.

Thunder rolling above is supposed to produce movement in the waters of the marsh below. The combination of this symbolism in Kuei Mei is recognized as an evil omen in the case which the name denotes. The application of it is not inappropriate.

CHEN, THUNDER
over
LI, FIRE

55   FENG; ABUNDANT PROSPERITY

THE TEXT:

Feng intimates progress and development. When a king has reached the point which the name denotes, there is no occasion to be anxious through fear of a change. Let him be as the sun at noon.

1. The first line, yang, shows its subject meeting with his mate. Though they are both of the same character, there will be no error. Advance will call forth approval.

2. The second line, yin, shows its subject surrounded by screens so large and thick that at midday he can see from them the constellation of the Bushel. If he go and try to enlighten his ruler who is thus emblemed, he will make himself to be viewed with suspicion and dislike. Let him cherish his feeling of sincere devotion that he may thereby move his ruler's mind, and there will be good fortune.

3. The third line, yang, shows its subject with an additional screen of a large and thick banner, through which at midday he can see the small Mei star. In the darkness he breaks his right arm; but there will be no error.

4. The fourth line, yang, shows its subject in a tent so large and thick that at midday he can see from it the constellation of the Bushel. But he meets with the

subject of the first line undivided like himself. There will be good fortune.

5. The fifth line, yin, shows its subject bringing around him the men of brilliant ability. There will be occasion for congratulation and praise. There will be good fortune.

6. The topmost line, yin, shows its subject with his house made large, but only serving as a screen to his household. When he looks at his door, it is still, and there is nobody about it. For three years no one is to be seen. There will be evil.

FROM THE WINGS:

Feng has the signification of being great. It is made up of the trigrams representing intelligence and movement directed by that intelligence. It is thus that it has that signification.

When the sun has reached the meridian height, it begins to decline. When the moon has become full, it begins to wane. The interaction of heaven and earth is now vigorous and abundant, now dull and scanty, growing and diminishing according to the seasons. How much more must it be so with the operations of men! How much more also with the spiritual agency!

The trigrams representing thunder and lightning combine to form Feng. The superior man, in accordance with this, decides cases of litigation, and apportions punishments with exactness.

1. "Though they are both of the same character, there will be no error": if the subject of this line seek to overpass that similarity, there will be calamity.

2. "Let him cherish his feeling of sincere devotion, that it shall appear being put forth": it is by sincerity that the mind is affected.

3. "There is an additional screen of a large and thick banner": great things should not be attempted in such circumstances.

"He breaks his right arm": in the end he will not be fit to be employed.

4. "He is surrounded by a screen large and thick": the position of the line is inappropriate.

"At midday he sees the constellation of the Bushel": there is darkness and no light.

"He meets with the subject of the line undivided like himself. There will be good fortune": action may be taken.

5. "The good fortune indicated by the fifth line, yin," is the congratulation that is sure to arise.

6. "He has made his house large": he soars in his pride to the heavens.

"He looks at his door, which is still, with no one about it": he only keeps himself withdrawn from all others.

FROM THE NOTES OF JAMES LEGGE:

The character Feng is the symbol of being large and abundant, and, as the name of this hexagram, denotes a condition of abundant prosperity. The component trigrams have the attributes of intelligence and of motive force, and the second is under the direction of the first. A ruler with these attributes is not likely to fail in maintaining his crown and prosperity, and it may well be said that the figure intimates progress and development.

The explanation of the T'uan is thus natural and easy. It will be found that a change is introduced in explaining the symbolism of the lines, which it is as well to point out here. Thus far we have found that to constitute a proper correlation between two lines, one of them must be whole and the other divided. Here two undivided lines make a correlation. The law, evidently made for the occasion, goes far to upset altogether the doctrine of correlated lines. There have been various deviations from them, but none so gross as that in this hexagram.

LI, FIRE
over
KEN, MOUNTAIN

56   LU; TRAVELING STRANGER

THE TEXT:

Lu intimates that in the condition which it denotes there may be some little attainment and progress. If the stranger or traveler be firm and correct as he ought to be, there will be good fortune.

1. The first line, yin, shows the stranger mean and meanly occupied. It is thus that he brings on himself further calamity.

2. The second line, yin, shows the stranger, occupying his lodging-house, carrying with him his means of livelihood, and provided with good and trusty servants.

3. The third line, yang, shows the stranger burning his lodging-house, and having lost his servants. However firm and correct he try to be, he will be in peril.

4. The fourth line, yang, shows the traveler in a resting-place, having also the means of livelihood and the ax, but still saying, "I am not at ease in my mind."

5. The fifth line, yin, shows its subject shooting a pheasant. He will lose his arrow, but in the end he will obtain praise and a high charge.

6. The sixth line, yang, suggests the idea of a bird burning its nest. The stranger, thus represented, first laughs and then cries out. He has lost his oxlike docility too readily and easily. There will be evil.

FROM THE WINGS:

"Lu indicates that there may be some small attainment and progress." We have also the attributes of quiet resting closely attached to intelligence in the component of trigrams. Hence it is said, "There may be some small attainment and progress. If the stranger or traveler be firm and correct as he ought to be, there will be good fortune."

Great is the time and great is the right course to be taken as intimated in Lu!

The trigram representing a mountain and above it that for fire form Lu. The superior man, in accordance with this, exerts his wisdom and caution in the use of punishments and not allowing litigations to continue.

1. "The stranger is mean and meanly occupied": his aim is become of the lowest character, and calamity will ensue.

2. "He is provided with good and trusty servants": he will in the end have nothing of which to complain.

3. "The stranger burns his lodging-house": and he himself also suffers hurt thereby. When, as a stranger, he treats those below him as the line indicates, the right relation between him and them is lost.

4. "The stranger is in a resting-place": but he has not got his proper position.

"He has the means of livelihood, and the ax": but his mind is not at ease.

5. "In the end he will obtain praise and a high charge": he has reached a high place.

6. "Considering that the stranger is here at the very height of distinction," with the spirit that possesses him, it is right he should be emblemed by a bird burning its nest. "He loses his oxlike docility too readily and eas-

ily": to the end he would not listen to the truth about the course to be pursued.

FROM THE NOTES OF JAMES LEGGE:

Different attempts are made to bring the idea of a traveling stranger out of the trigrams Ken and Li; but none of them is satisfactory. Let K'ung Ying-ta's view serve as a specimen of them: "A fire on a mountain lays hold of the grass, and runs with it over the whole space, not stopping anywhere long, and soon disappearing; such is the emblem of the traveler."

When an officer was traveling abroad in ancient times, his gift of introduction at any feudal court was a pheasant.

SUN, WIND
Repeated

57 SUN; THE PENETRATING

THE TEXT:

Sun intimates that under the conditions which it denotes there will be some little attainment and progress. There will be advantage in movement onward in whatever direction. It will be advantageous also to see the great man.

1. The first line, yin, shows its subject now advancing, now receding. It would be advantageous for him to have the firm correctness of a brave soldier.

2. The second line, yang, shows the representative of Sun beneath a couch, and employing diviners and exorcists in a way bordering on confusion. There will be good fortune and no error.

3. The third line, yang, shows its subject penetrating only by violent and repeated efforts. There will be occasion for regret.

4. The fourth line, yin, shows all occasion for repentance in its subject passed away. He takes game for its threefold use in his hunting.

5. The fifth line, yang, shows that with firm correctness there will be good fortune. All occasion for repentance will disappear; all movements will be advantageous. There may have been no good beginning, but there will be a good end. Three days before making any changes, let him give notice of them; and three

days after, let him reconsider them. There will thus be good fortune.

6. The sixth line, yang, shows the representative of penetration beneath a couch, and having lost the ax with which he executed his decisions. However firm and correct he may try to be, there will be evil.

FROM THE WINGS:

The double Sun shows how, in accordance with it, governmental orders are reiterated.

We see that the strong fifth line has penetrated into the central and correct place, and the will of its subject is being carried into effect; we see also the first and fourth lines, yin, obedient to the strong lines above them. It is hence said, "There will be some little attainment and progress. There will be advantage in movement onward in whatever direction. It will be advantageous also to see the great man.

Two trigrams representing wind, following each other, form Sun. The superior man, in accordance with this, reiterates his orders and secures the practice of his affairs.

1. "Now he advances, now he recedes": his mind is perplexed.

"It would be advantageous for him to have the firmness of a brave soldier": his mind would in that case be well governed.

2. "The good fortune springing from what borders on confusion" is due to the position of the line in the center.

3. "The regret arising from the violent and repeated efforts to penetrate" shows the exhaustion of the will.

4. "He takes game in his hunting, enough for the three-fold use of it": he achieves merit.

5. "The good fortune of the subject of the fifth line, yang," is owing to its correct position and its being in the center.

6. "The representative of penetration is beneath a couch": though occupying the topmost place, his powers are exhausted.

"He has lost the ax with which he executed his decisions": though he try to be correct, there will be evil.

FROM THE NOTES OF JAMES LEGGE:

In this hexagram we are to think of it as representing wind with its penetrating power, finding its way into every corner and cranny.

Confucius once said (Analects 12. 19): "The relation between superiors and inferiors is like that between the wind and the grass. The grass must bend when the wind blows upon it."

The evil that paragraph 6 concludes with would arise from the quality of Sun being carried to excess.

TUI, MARSH
Repeated

58 TUI; PLEASURE

THE TEXT:

Tui intimates that under its conditions there will be progress and attainment. But it will be advantageous to be firm and correct.

1. The first line, yang, shows the pleasure of inward harmony. There will be good fortune.

2. The second line, yang, shows the pleasure arising from inward sincerity. There will be good fortune. Occasion for repentance will disappear.

3. The third line, yin, shows its subject bringing round himself whatever can give pleasure. There will be evil.

4. The fourth line, yang, shows its subject deliberating about what to seek his pleasure in, and not at rest. He borders on what would be injurious, but there will be cause for joy.

5. The fifth line, yang, shows its subject trusting in one who would injure him. The situation is perilous.

6. The topmost line, yin, shows the pleasure of its subject in leading and attracting others.

FROM THE WINGS:

Tui has the meaning of pleased satisfaction.

In pleasure what is most advantageous is the maintenance of firm correctness. Through this there will be found an accordance with the will of heaven, and a correspondence with the feelings of men. When such pleasure goes before the people and leads them on, they forget their toils; when it animates them in encountering difficulties, they forget the risk of death. How great is the power of this pleased satisfaction, stimulating in such a way the people!

Two symbols representing the waters of a marsh, one over the other, form Tui. The superior man, in accordance with this, encourages the conversation of friends and the stimulus of their common practice.

1. "The good fortune attached to the pleasure of inward harmony" arises from there being nothing in the conduct of the subject of the line to awaken doubt.

2. "The good fortune attached to the pleasure arising from inward sincerity" is due to the confidence felt in the object of the subject of the line.

3. "The evil predicated of one's bringing around himself whatever can give pleasure" is shown by the inappropriateness of the place of the line.

4. "The joy in connection with the subject of the fourth line, yang," is due to the happiness which he will produce.

5. "He trusts in one who would injure him": his place is that which is correct and appropriate.

6. "The topmost line, yin, shows the pleasure of its subject in leading and attracting others": his virtue is not yet brilliant.

FROM THE NOTES OF JAMES LEGGE:

The K'ang Hsi editors say: "When the airs of spring begin to blow, from the collections of water on the earth the moistening vapors rise up and descend again; so, when the breath of health is vigorous in a man's person, the hue of it is displayed in his complexion. Akin to this is the significance of the hexagram Tui representing a marsh, as denoting pleasure. Although the yin lines give it its special character, they owe their power and effect to the yang; so when the qualities of mildness and harmony prevail in a man, without true-heartedness and integrity to control and direct them, they will fail to be correct, and may degenerate into what is evil. Hence it is said that it will be advantageous to be firm and correct!"

The feeling then of pleasure is the subject of this hexagram.

SUN, WIND
over
K'AN, WATER

59   HUAN; DISPERSION

THE TEXT:

Huan intimates that under its conditions there will be progress and success. The king goes to his ancestral temple; and it will be advantageous to cross the great stream. It will be advantageous to be firm and correct.

1. The first line, yin, shows its subject engaged in rescuing from the impending evil and having the assistance of a strong horse. There will be good fortune.

2. The second line, yang, shows its subject, amid the dispersion, hurrying to his contrivance for security. All occasion for repentance will disappear.

3. The third line, yin, shows its subject discarding any regard to his own person. There will be no occasion for repentance.

4. The fourth line, yin, shows its subject scattering the different parties in the state, which leads to great good fortune. From the dispersion he collects again good men standing out, a crowd like a mound, which is what ordinary men would not have thought of.

5. The fifth line, yang, shows its subject amidst the dispersion issuing his great announcements as the perspiration flows from his body. He scatters abroad also the accumulations in the royal granaries. There will be no error.

6. The topmost line, yang, shows its subject disposing of what may be called bloody wounds, and going and separating himself from its anxious fears. There will be no error.

FROM THE WINGS:

"Huan intimates that there will be progress and success."

"The king goes to his ancestral temple": the king's mind is without any deflection.

"It will be advantageous to cross the great stream": the subject of the hexagram rides in a vessel of wood over water, and will do so with success.

The trigram representing water and that for wind moving above the water form Huan. The ancient kings, in accordance with this, presented offerings to God and established the ancestral temple.

1. "The good fortune attached to the first line, yin," is due to the natural course pursued by its subject.

2. "Amidst the prevailing dispersion, he hurries to his contrivance for security": he gets what he desires.

3. "He has no regard to his own person": his aim is directed to what is external to himself.

4. "He scatters the different parties in the state, and there is great good fortune": brilliant and great are his virtue and service.

5. "The accumulations of the royal granaries are dispersed, and there is no error": this is due to the correctness of the position.

6. "His bloody wounds are gone": he is far removed from the danger of injury.

FROM THE NOTES OF JAMES LEGGE:

"The symbol of water and that of wind above it form

Huan. The ancient kings, in accordance with this, presented offerings to God, and established the ancestral temple." The union of the two trigrams suggested to king Wen the idea of dissipation in the alienation of men from the Supreme Power, and of the minds of parents from their children; a condition which the wisdom of the ancient kings saw could best be met by the influences of religion.

The "in accordance with this" must be equivalent to "to remedy the state of things thus symbolized." What follows certainly amounts to this, that the ancient kings considered the services of religion, sincerely and earnestly attended to, as calculated to counteract the tendency to mutual alienation and selfishness in the minds of men. How they operated to have this beneficial effect we are not told. Nor is it easy to account for the extension of what is said in the Text about the establishment of the ancestral temple to the presentation also of offerings to God.

Huan, the name of this hexagram, denotes a state of dissipation or dispersion; primarily of men's minds alienated from what is right and good. This alienation is sure to go on to disorder in the commonwealth; and an attempt is made to show how it should be dealt with and remedied.

The upper trigram Sun represents both wind and wood. To explain the meaning of Huan, the significance of wind is taken; the writer here seizes on that of wood, as furnishing materials for a boat in which the great stream can be crossed.

K'AN, WATER
over
TUI, MARSH

60 CHIEH; JUST REGULATIONS

THE TEXT:

Chieh intimates that under its conditions there will be progress and attainment. If the regulations which it prescribes be severe and difficult, they cannot be permanent.

1. The first line, yang, shows its subject not quitting the courtyard outside his door. There will be no error.

2. The second line, yang, shows its subject not quitting the courtyard inside his gate. There will be evil.

3. The third line, yin, shows its subject with no appearance of observing the proper regulations, in which case we shall see him lamenting. But there will be no one to blame but himself.

4. The fourth line, yin, shows its subject quietly and naturally attentive to all regulations. There will be progress and success.

5. The fifth line, yang, shows its subject sweetly and acceptably enacting his regulations. There will be good fortune. The onward progress with them will afford ground for admiration.

6. The topmost line, yin, shows its subject enacting regulations severe and difficult. Even with firmness and correctness there will be evil. But though there will be cause for repentance, it will by and by disappear.

FROM THE WINGS:

"Chieh intimates progress and attainment": the yang and yin lines are equally divided, and the strong lines occupy the central places.

"If the regulations be severe and difficult, they cannot be permanent": its course of action will in that case come to an end.

We have the feeling of pleasure and satisfaction directing the course amidst peril. We have all regulations controlled by authority in its proper place. We have free action proceeding from the central and correct position.

Heaven and earth observe their regular terms, and we have the four seasons complete. If rulers frame their measures according to the due regulations, the resources of the state suffer no injury, and the people receive no hurt.

The trigram representing a lake, and above it that for water, form Chieh. The superior man, in accordance with this, constructs his methods of numbering and measurement, and discusses points of virtue and conduct.

1. "He does not quit the courtyard outside his door": he knows when he has free course and when he is obstructed.

2. "He does not quit the courtyard inside his gate. There will be evil": he loses the time for action to an extreme degree.

3. In "the lamentation for not observing the proper regulations," who should there be to blame?

4. "The progress and success of the quiet and natural attention to all regulations" is due to the deference which accepts the ways of the ruler above.

5. "The good fortune arising from the regulations enacted sweetly and acceptably" is due to the line occupying the place of authority and being in the center.

6. "The regulations are severe and difficult. Even with firm correctness there will be evil": the course indicated by the hexagram is come to an end.

FROM THE NOTES OF JAMES LEGGE:

The primary application of the character Chieh was to denote the joints of the bamboo; it is used also for the joints of the human frame; and for the solar and other terms of the year. Whatever makes regular division may be denominated a Chieh. There enter into it the ideas of regulating and restraining; and the subject of this hexagram is the regulations of government enacted for the guidance and control of the people.

SUN, WIND
over
TUI, MARSH

61 CHUNG FU; INMOST SINCERITY

THE TEXT:

Chung Fu moves even pigs and fish, and leads to
good fortune. There will be advantage in crossing the
great stream. There will be advantage in being firm
and correct.

1. The first line, yang, shows its subject resting in
himself. There will be good fortune. If he sought any
other, he would not find rest.

2. The second line, yang, shows its subject like the
crane crying out in her hidden retirement, and her
young ones responding to her. It is as if it were said,
"I have a cup of good spirits," and the response were,
"I will partake of it with you."

3. The third line, yin, shows its subject having met
with his mate. Now he beats his drum, and now he
leaves off. Now he weeps, and now he sings.

4. The fourth line, yin, shows its subject like the moon
nearly full, and like a horse in a chariot whose fellow
disappears. There will be no error.

5. The fifth line, yang, shows its subject perfectly
sincere, and linking others to him in closest union. There
will be no error.

6. The topmost line, yang, shows its subject in chanticleer trying to mount to heaven. Even with firm correctness there will be evil.

FROM THE WINGS:

We have the attributes of pleased satisfaction and flexible penetration. Sincerity thus symboled will transform a country.

"Pigs and fish are moved, and there will be good fortune": sincerity reaches to and affects even pigs and fishes.

"There will be advantage in crossing the great stream": we see in the figure one riding on the emblem of wood, which forms an empty boat.

In the exercise of the virtue denoted by Chung Fu, it is said that "there will be advantage in being firm and correct": in that virtue indeed we have the response of man to Heaven.

The trigram representing the waters of a marsh and that for wind above it form Chung Fu. The superior man, in accordance with this, deliberates about cases of litigation and delays the infliction of death.

1. The first line, yang, shows it subject resting in himself. There will be good fortune": no change has yet come over his purpose.

2. "Her young ones respond to her": from the common wish of the inmost heart.

3. "Now he beats his drum, and now he leaves off": the position of the line is the appropriate one for it.

4. "A horse the fellow of which disappears": he breaks from his former companions and mounts upward.

5. "He is perfectly sincere, and links others to him in closest union": the place of the line is the correct and appropriate one.

6. "Chanticleer tries to mount to heaven": but how can such an effort continue long?

FROM THE NOTES OF JAMES LEGGE:

Chung Fu may be represented in English by "Inmost Sincerity." It denotes the highest quality of man, and gives its possessor power so that he prevails with spiritual beings, with other men, and with the lower creatures.

The lineal figure has suggested to the Chinese commentators two ideas in it which deserve to be pointed out. There are two divided lines in the center and two undivided below them and above them. The divided lines are held to represent the heart or mind free from all preoccupation, without any consciousness of self; the undivided lines are held to denote the solidity of the virtue of one so free from selfishness. There is no unreality in it, not a single flaw.

The authors give no instance of the affecting of "pigs and fishes" by sincerity, and say that these names are symbolical of men, the rudest and most unsusceptible of being acted on. The Text says that the man thus gifted with sincerity will succeed in the most difficult of enterprises. Remarkable is the concluding sentence that he must be firm and correct. Here, as elsewhere throughout the I, there comes out the practical character which has distinguished the Chinese people and their best teaching all along the line of history.

The K'ang Hsi editors say: "The wind penetrates things. The grass and trees of the level ground are shaken and tossed by it; the rocky valleys and caverns in their sides have it blowing round about them; and it acts also on the depths of the collected waters, the cold of which disappears and the ice is melted before it. This is what makes it the emblem of that perfect sincerity which penetrates everywhere. The litigations of the people are like the deep and dark places of the earth. The kings examine with discrimination into all secret matters connected with them, even those which are here mentioned, till there is nothing that is not penetrated by their perfect sincerity."

CHEN, THUNDER
over
KEN, MOUNTAIN

62   HSIAO KUO; SMALL EXCESSES

THE TEXT:

Hsiao Kuo indicates that in the circumstances which it implies there will be progress and attainment. But it will be advantageous to be firm and correct. What the name denotes may be done in small affairs but not in great affairs. It is like the notes that come down from a bird on the wing; to descend is better than to ascend. There will in this way be great good fortune.

1. The first line, yin, suggests the idea of a bird flying, and ascending till the issue is evil.

2. The second line, yin, shows its subject passing by his grandfather and meeting with his grandmother; not attempting anything against his ruler but meeting him as his minister. There will be no error.

3. The third line, yang, shows its subject taking no extraordinary precautions against danger; and some in consequence finding opportunity to assail and injure him. There will be evil.

4. The fourth line, yang, shows its subject falling into no error, but meeting the exigency of his situation, without exceeding in his natural course. If he go forward, there will be peril, and he must be cautious. There is no occasion to be using firmness perpetually.

5. The fifth line, yin, suggests the idea of dense

clouds, but no rain, coming from our borders in the west. It also shows the prince shooting his arrow, and taking the bird in a cave.

6. The sixth line, yin, shows its subject not meeting the exigency of his situation, and exceeding his proper course. It suggests the idea of a bird flying far aloft. There will be evil. The case is what is called one of calamity and self-produced injury.

FROM THE WINGS:

In Hsiao Kuo we see the small lines exceeding the others, and giving the intimation of progress and attainment.

Such "exceeding must be associated with firmness and correctness": that is, it must take place only according to the requirements of the time.

The yin lines are in the central places, and hence it is said that what the name denotes may be done in small affairs, and there will be good fortune. Of the yang lines one is not in its proper place and the other is not central, hence it is said that what the name denotes "should not be done in great affairs."

In the hexagram we have "the symbol of a bird on the wing, and of the notes that come down from such a bird, for which it is better to descend than to ascend, thereby leading to great good fortune": to ascend is contrary to what is reasonable in the case, while to descend is natural and right.

The trigram representing a hill and that for thunder above it form Hsiao Kuo. The superior man, in accordance with this, in his conduct exceeds in humility, in mourning exceeds in sorrow, and in his expenditure exceeds in economy.

1. There is a bird flying and ascending till the result is evil": nothing can be done to avoid this issue.

2. "He does not attempt to reach his ruler": a minister should not overpass the distance between his ruler and himself.

3. "Some in consequence find opportunity to assail and injure him. There will be evil": how great will it be!

4. "He meets the exigency of his situation, without exceeding the proper course": he does so, the position being inappropriate for a yang line.

"If he go forward, there will be peril, and he must be cautious": the result would be that his course would not be long pursued.

5. "There are dense clouds but no rain": the line is in too high a place.

6. "He does not meet the exigency of his situation, and exceeds his proper course": the position indicates the habit of domineering.

From the Notes of James Legge:

The name Hsiao Kuo is explained both by reference to the lines of the hexagram, and to the meaning of the characters. The explanation from the lines appears immediately on comparing them with those of Ta Kuo, the 28th hexagram. There the first and sixth lines are divided, and between are four undivided lines; here the third and fourth lines are undivided, and outside each of them are two divided lines. The undivided or yang lines are great, the divided or yin lines are called small. In Hsiao Kuo the divided or small lines predominate.

This peculiar structure of the figure could be of no interest to the student if it were not for the meaning of the name, which is "small excesses" or "exceeding in what is small." The author, accepted by us as king Wen, had in his mind our distinction of essentials and nonessentials. Is it ever good to deviate from what is recognized as the established course of procedure? The reply is—never in the matter of right; but in what is conventional and ceremonial, in what is nonessential, the deviation may be made, and will be productive of good. The form may be given up, but not the substance. But the thing must be done very carefully, humbly and reverently, and in small matters.

The symbolism of the bird is intended to teach humility. It is better for the bird to descend, keeping near to where it can perch and rest, than to hold on ascending into the homeless regions of the air.

K'AN, WATER
over
LI, FIRE

63 CHI CHI; SUCCESSFUL ACCOMPLISHMENT

THE TEXT:

Chi Chi intimates progress and success in small matters. There will be advantage in being firm and correct. There has been good fortune in the beginning; there may be disorder in the end.

1. The first line, yang, shows its subject as a driver who drags back his wheel, or as a fox which has wet its tail. There will be no error.

2. The second line, yin, shows its subject as a wife who has lost her carriage-screens. There is no occasion to go in pursuit of it. In seven days she will find it.

3. The third line, yang, suggests the case of Kao Chung who attacked the Demon region, but was three years in subduing it. Small men should not be employed in such enterprises.

4. The fourth line, yin, shows its subject with rags provided against any leak in his boat, and on his guard all day long.

5. The fifth line, yang, shows its subject as the neighbor in the east who slaughters an ox for his sacrifice; but this is not equal to the small spring sacrifice of the neighbor in the west, whose sincerity receives the blessing.

6. The topmost line, yin, shows its subject with even his head immersed. The position is perilous.

From the Wings:

"Chi Chi intimates progress and success": in small matters, that is, there will be that progress and success.

"There will be advantage in being firm and correct": the yang and yin lines are correctly arranged, each in its appropriate place.

"There has been good fortune in the beginning": the second line, yin, is in the center.

"In the end" there is a cessation of effort, and "disorder arises": the course that led to rule and order is now exhausted.

The trigram representing fire and that for water above it form Chi Chi. The superior man, in accordance with this, thinks of evil that may come, and beforehand guards against it.

3. "He drags back his wheel": as we may rightly judge, there will be no mistake.

2. "In seven days she will find it": for the course pursued is that indicated by the central position of the line.

3. "He was three years in subduing it": enough to make him weary.

4. "He is on his guard all the day": he is in doubt about something.

5. "The slaughtering of an ox by the neighbor in the east is not equal to the small sacrifice of the neighbor in the west": because the time in the latter case is more important and fit.

"His sincerity receives the blessing": good fortune comes on a great scale.

6. "His head is immersed; the position is perilous": how could such a state continue long?

FROM THE NOTES OF JAMES LEGGE:

The characters used to symbol Chi Chi express the successful accomplishment of whatever the writer has in his mind. In dealing with this lineal figure, king Wen was thinking of the condition of the kingdom, at length at rest and quiet. The vessel of the state has been brought safely across the great and dangerous stream. The distresses of the kingdom have been relieved, and its disorders have been repressed. Does anything remain to be done still? Yes, in small things. The new government has to be consolidated. Its ruler must, without noise or clamor, go on to perfect what has been wrought, with firmness and correctness, and ever keeping in mind the instability of all human affairs. That every line of the hexagram is in its correct place, and has its proper correlate is also supposed to harmonize with the intimation of progress and success.

LI, FIRE
over
K'AN, WATER

64 WEI CHI; MORE TO DO

THE TEXT:

Wei Chi intimates progress and success in the circumstances which it implies. We see a young fox that has nearly crossed the stream, when its tail gets immersed. There will be no advantage in any way.

1. The first line, yin, shows its subject like a fox whose tail gets immersed. There will be occasion for regret.

2. The second line, yang, shows its subject dragging back his carriage-wheel. With firmness and correctness there will be good fortune.

3. The third line, yin, shows its subject, with the state of things not yet remedied, advancing on; which will lead to evil. But there will be advantage in trying to cross the great stream.

4. The fourth line, yang, shows its subject by firm correctness obtaining good fortune, so that all occasion for repentance disappears. Let him stir himself up, as if he were invading the Demon region, where for three years rewards will come to him and his troops from the great kingdom.

5. The fifth line, yin, shows its subject by firm correctness obtaining good fortune, and having no occasion for repentance. We see in him the brightness of a superior man, and the possession of sincerity. There will be good fortune.

6. The topmost line, yang, shows its subject full of confidence and therefore feasting quietly. There will be no error. If he cherish this confidence, till he is like the fox who gets his head immersed, it will fail of what is right.

FROM THE WINGS:

"Wei Chi intimates progress and success in the circumstances which it implies": the fifth line, yin, is in the center.

"The young fox has nearly crossed the stream": but he has not yet escaped from the midst of the danger and calamity.

"Its tail gets immersed. There will be no advantage in any way": there is not at the end a continuance of the purpose at the beginning. Although the places of the different lines are not those appropriate to them, yet a yang line and a yin line always respond to each other.

The trigram representing water and that for fire above it form Wei Chi. The superior man, in accordance with this, carefully discriminates among the qualities of things, and the different positions they naturally occupy.

1. "His tail gets immersed": this is the very height of ignorance.

2. "The second line, yang, shows good fortune arising from being firm and correct": it is in the central place, and the action of its subject thereby becomes correct.

3. "The state of things is not yet remedied. Advancing will lead to evil": the place of the line is not that appropriate for it.

4. "By firm correctness there is good fortune, and cause for repentance disappears": the aim of the subject of the line is carried into effect.

5. "We see the brightness of a superior man": the diffusion of that brightness tends to good fortune.

6. "He drinks and gets his head immersed": he does not know how to submit to the proper regulations.

FROM THE NOTES OF JAMES LEGGE:

Wei Chi is the reverse of Chi Chi. The name tells us that the successful accomplishment of whatever the writer had in his mind had not yet been realized. The vessel of the state has not been brought across the great and dangerous stream. Some have wished that the I might have concluded with Chi Chi, and the last hexagram have left us with the picture of human affairs all brought to good order. But this would not have been in harmony with the idea of the I as the book of change. Again and again it has been pointed out that we find in it no idea of a perfect and abiding state. Just as the seasons of the year change and pursue an ever-recurring round, so is it with the phases of society. The reign of order has been, and has terminated; and this hexagram calls us to see the struggle for its realization recommenced. It treats of how those engaged in that struggle should conduct themselves with a view to secure the happy consummation.

Thus of the diagrams some are small, and some are great. Of the explanations some are startling and some are unexciting.

The appellations and names of the diagrams and lines are but small matters, but the classes of things comprehended under them are large. Their scope reaches far, and the explanations attached to them are elegant. The words are indirect but to the point. The matters seem plainly set forth, but there is a secret principle in them. Their object is, in cases that are doubtful, to help the people in their conduct, and to make plain the recompenses of good and evil.

The numbering of the past is a natural process; the knowledge of the coming is anticipation. Therefore in the I we have both anticipation and the natural process.

The I exhibits the past, and teaches us to discriminate the issues of the future. It makes manifest what is minute and brings to light what is obscure. Then king Wen opened its symbols and distinguished things in accordance with its names, so that all his words were correct and his explanations decisive. The book is now complete.

C
H
A
CHANGES
G
E
S

from the *I Ching Book of Changes*
translated by
James Legge

HEXAGRAMS IN ALPHABETICAL ORDER

THE HEXAGRAMS IN ALPHABETICAL ORDER

I CHING

Wade-Giles	Yale System	Name of Hexagram	No.
Li	(Li)	Double Brightness	30
Lin	(Lin)	Authority Comes	19
Lu	(Lyu)	Walk Softly	10
Lu	(Lyu)	Traveling Stranger	56
Meng	(Meng)	Youth	4
Ming I	(Ming Yi)	Intelligence Repressed	36
Pi	(Bi)	Union	8
Pi	(Bi)	Adornment	22
P'i	(Pi)	The Waning	12
Po	(Bwo)	Overthrow	23
Sheng	(Sheng)	Advance	46
Shih	(Shr)	Hosts	7
Shih Ho	(Shr He)	Union by Gnawing	21
Sui	(Swei)	Following	17
Sun	(Swun)	Payment Due	41
Sun	(Swun)	The Penetrating	57
Sung	(Sung)	Strife	6
Ta Chuang	(Da Jwang)	Abundant Strength	34
T'ai	(Tai)	The Waxing	11
Ta Kuo	(Da Gwo)	Greatness and Difficulty	28
Ta Ch'u	(Da Chu)	Great Accumulation	26
Ta Yu	(Da You)	Great Havings	14
Ting	(Ding)	Cauldron	50
Tui	(Dwei)	Pleasure	58
Tun	(Dwun)	Seclusion	33
Ts'ui	(Tswei)	Gatherings	45
T'ung Jen	(Tung Ren)	Brotherhood	13
Wei Chi	(Wei Ji)	More to Do	64
Wu Wang	(Wu Wang)	Sincerity	25
Yu	(You)	Harmony	16

HEXAGRAM LOCATER

The upper trigram being	CH'IEN	TUI	LI	CHEN	K'UN	KEN	K'AN	SUN
1 CH'IEN, Heaven, the yang principle, with	1	43	14	34	11	26	5	9
2 TUI, Marsh, symboling happiness	10	58	38	54	19	41	60	61
3 LI, Fire, symboling brightness	13	49	30	55	36	22	63	37
4 CHEN, Thunder, symboling exciting power	25	17	21	51	24	27	3	42
5 K'UN, Earth, the yin principle	12	45	35	16	2	23	8	20
6 KEN, Mountain, both the active and the passive	33	31	56	62	15	52	39	53
7 K'AN, Water, which symbols both Water and Peril	6	47	64	40	7	4	29	59
8 SUN, Wind - Wood, the penetrating and the flexible	44	28	50	32	46	18	48	57

ALPHABETICAL REFERENCE

When definitions are drawn from the translation, or are in the words of James Legge, they are followed by the initials J. L. within parentheses.

Some terms not overtly connected with the text are given because they are illustrative of the spherical nature of thought within the *I Ching*. A few references are made for historical purposes.

One must remain alert to the many homophonic words in Chinese, such as *jen*—which signifies both a man and also humanity, as well as a state of benevolent perfection.

Names of personages appear in capital letters; proper
nouns are capitalized; all other references are lower case.
NOTE: Chinese words and names given in Wade-Giles
system are followed by the Yale system within parentheses: to aid pronunciation.

advantageous

What is called "the advantageous" is the harmony of all
that is right. (J.L.)

ai (ai)

love which encompasses the four Western aspects of
agape, eros, philia and *caritas*.

antiquity, periods of

high antiquity begins with Fu Hsi, B.C. 3322; middle,
with the rise of the Chou dynasty, B.C. 1122; lowest antiquity
is dated from the Confucian era of the sixth century B.C.
(J.L.)

anxiety

In addition to our meaning of the word, in Chinese
thought a moral sense: anxiety, the wisdom of the *I* informs
us, should be felt at the boundary line between good and
evil. (J.L.)

belly

is representative of the inner self, or synonymous with
the unconscious.
"Belly of the dark land" (Hexagram 36, Line 4) is a
symbolic way of speaking of an idea of the inward mind.

benevolence and righteousness

What is possible for man; hence, lines 3 and 4 of the
hexagram consulted.

buff-coat and helmet

symbols of the military man.

Bushel, the
   Ursa Major. Anciently, this constellation was much closer to the North Pole, described a narrower path in its orbits, and was endowed with mystical aspects.

buttocks
   Legge remarks that the buttocks is a symbol much used by the duke of Chou, but dismisses it with a "chacun à son goût."

ch'an (chan)
   contemplation. In Japan it became known as Zen.

change—changes—course of things
   ". . . a door shut may be pronounced analogous to K'un or the inactive condition, and the opening of the door analogous to Ch'ien, or the active condition. The opening succeeding the being shut may be pronounced analogous to what we call a change; and the passing from one of these states to the other may be called the constant course of things." (J.L.)

Chen (Jen)
   trigram of *Thunder*:

repeated, forms hexagram	51:	Chen (Jen)
with K'un above forms hexagram	24:	Fu (Fu)
with Ken above forms hexagram	27:	I (Yi)
with K'an above forms hexagram	3:	Chun (Jwun)
with Sun above forms hexagram	42:	I (Yi)
with Ch'ien above forms hexagram	25:	Wu Wang (Wu Wang)
with Tui above forms hexagram	17:	Sui (Swei)
with Li above forms hexagram	21:	Shih Ho (Shr He)

chen ku (jen gu)
   firm correctness, and all that may be associated with the superior man.

cheng (jeng)
   what is seemly, and normal; what is righteous, and beneficial.

CHENG K'ANG CH'ENG (JENG KANG CHENG)
Scholar, interpreter of the *I*. Legge, when confronted by corruptions of text or conflicting interpretations, relied heavily on his judgment. A.D. 127-200.

Ch'ien (Chyan)
    trigram of *Heaven*:

repeated, forms hexagram	1:	Ch'ien (Chyan)
with Tui above forms hexagram	43:	Kuai (Gwai)
with Li above forms hexagram	14:	Ta Yu (Da You)
with Chen above forms hexagram	34:	Ta Chuang (Da Chwang)
with K'un above forms hexagram	11:	T'ai (Tai)
with Ken above forms hexagram	26:	Ta Ch'u (Da Chu)
with K'an above forms hexagram	5:	Hsu (Syu)
with Sun above forms hexagram	9:	Hsiau Ch'u (Syau Chu)

Ch'in (Chin) dynasty:
    B.C. 249-206; succeeded by the Han dynasty.

ch'ing (ching)
    refers to emotional states, of which seven are categorized:
    1. anger
    2. desire
    3. fear
    4. hatred
    5. joy
    6. love
    7. sorrow

CHOU (JOU), duke of
    Author of the yao: explanations of the lines of the hexagrams which follow king Wen's opening paragraph (the t'uan), and which are numbered 1 through 6. Died B.C. 1105.

Chou (Jou) dynasty:
    succeeded the Shang dynasty; king Wen and the duke of Chou were its earliest leaders. In B.C. 249 it was succeeded by the Ch'in dynasty.

CHU CHEN (JU JEN)
Sung dynasty scholar admired by Legge.

CHU HSI (JU SYI)
A Sung dynasty commentator on the classics. His decisions influenced future interpretations. Author of *Lessons on the I for the Young.* A.D. 1130-1200.

Ch'un Ch'iu (Chwun Chyou)
Spring and Autumn Annals, one of the five classics.

chun tzu (jwun dz)
a sagely man.

chung (jung)
sincerity and honesty in all one's dealings.

colors:
   azure — symbol of heaven and hence of Ch'ien
   black — symbol of the yin force
   purple — sky
   white — simplicity
   yellow — earth, and hence of K'un
      one of the five "correct" colors, hence good auspice
      can symbolize "the correct course"
   mixtures: azure and yellow—heaven and earth
      purple and yellow—earth and sky

conditions presupposed, etc.
In the t'uan of king Wen, one meets the restrictive phrase "in the condition which (the hexagram) supposes" or presupposes . . . Legge warns us this is indicative of a particular reference to specific situations; the modern reader must abstract the meaning to find current applications.

CONFUCIUS
Also known as Ch'iu, K'ung, K'ung Ch'iu, Chung-ni, K'ung-Fe-Tse. B.C. 550-478.

course of things
The successive movement of the inactive and active

operations constitutes what is called the course of things. (J.L.)

This is another way to speak of tao. In the earliest components of the *I* the word tao is seldom used. It would be a mistake, however, to assume that it wasn't recognized because it wasn't named. Taoism as a school of thought did not develop until the Fifth Century B.C.

divination, the 12 tokens method (6 light, 6 dark)

From a box or other receptacle select a token without conscious knowledge of whether it is light or dark. Place it on a surface close to you, leaving ample space above. This is line 1 of the hexagram you are forming; the bottom line.

If you have placed before you a light token, on a piece of paper draw an undivided, yang, line.

If you have placed before you a dark token, on your paper draw a divided line, yin.

Repeat this operation five times, placing the tokens in ascending order, numbering the lines up to 6, the topmost line.

Transcribe onto your paper appropriate symbols above the one you already have there, the first. Undivided, yang, lines symbol the light tokens; divided, yin, lines symbol the dark tokens.

You now have drawn six lines, completing the structure of the hexagram you will consult.

Taking care to assign the correct number to the hexagram you have formed, you are now ready to read the explanation as given in the text.

(This summarizes the method given on pages 91-95.)

a door open

from the concept of Ch'ien; what penetrates and originates; what is inspired, what is creative.

a door shut

from the concept of K'un; a vast capacity; responsiveness; growth and gestation, what is receptive.

dragon

It has been from the earliest time the emblem with the Chinese of the highest dignity and wisdom, of sovereignty and sagehood, the combination of which constitutes "the great man." (J.L.)

error
"There will be no error" indicates the subject will repair an error by means of what is good. (J.L.)

evil
indicates unlucky rather than immoral.

fa (fa)
has the meaning of both legal and of law in its most exalted sense. It also can refer to Buddhism, Buddhist.

fires of Ch'in (Chin)
the burning of books in B.C. 213 ordered by Shih Huang Ti. Legge describes this as disastrous to most of the ancient literature. The *I Ching* escaped, along with a few others, as books on husbandry, medicine, and divination were excepted.

firm correctness
firm correctness is integrity, and to maintain one's integrity when tempted. What is called the "correct and firm" is the faculty of action.

five classics:
sometimes called the *Sacred Books*:
1. *Shu Ching* (Shu Jing)   — *Book of History*
2. *Shih Ching* (Shr Jing)   — *Book of Poetry*
3. *I Ching* (Yi Jing)   — *Book of Changes*
4. *Ch'un Ch'iu* (Chwun Chyou) — *Spring and Autumn Annals*
5. *Li Chi* (Li Ji)   — *Book of Rites*

Five dynasties, the
from A.D. 907 to 960. It was during this period that block printing was invented.

Five Sages, Period of
from Fu Hsi, B.C. 3400, to Shun, B.C. 2200.

follow
"To be followed": indicates success. If no one will follow, it denotes lack of success.

four emblematic symbols
see hsiang.

FU HSI (Fu Syi)
inventor of the Eight Trigrams; 34th century B.C.

Grand Terminus
see T'ai Chi.

Great Expansion
see T'ai Chi.

Great Extreme
see T'ai Chi.

great stream, crossing—going through, etc.
may mean undertaking hazardous enterprises, encountering difficulties, or assuming large responsibility. Sometimes it has a geographical meaning: Yellow River.

Han (Han) dynasty:
B.C. 206 to A.D. 221. Under the Hans paper was invented. Travel, exploration, and foreign trade flourished.
In the early part of this dynasty, scholars sought to replace the books which had disappeared in the fires of Chin. Searches of walls and other hidden caches were instituted. Texts which had been lost to all but memory were again committed to writing.

HO, the . . . cross the Ho:
this refers to the Yellow River.

horns
a symbol of strength; wood over horns (as in Hexagram 26) a symbol of caution.

hosts
"The hosts" is a term frequently used, and in the sense of population; or "the people"—meaning "citizens."

Hsia (Sya) dynasty:
B.C. 2197-1766. China's first historic dynasty, about which little is known. Succeeded by Shang dynasty.

hsiang (syang)
literally, image. Interpretations of the lines of the hexagrams which, collectively, are called the yao.

hsiang (syang)
is the name given to the four emblematic symbols called the old and young yang, old and young yin. This represents the first coupling of the yang with the yin; the next manipulation resulted in the eight trigrams.

hsiao (syau)
a stroke of the hexagram, of which there are six to each figure.

hsin (syin)
holding the attributes of, or faithfully practicing, the highest forms of human decency in all activities.

HUANG TI (HWANG DI)
a legendary emperor, succeeded Shen Nung.

humility
one of the virtues mentioned again and again in the *I*. The phrase "adds humility to humility" indicates one who nourishes his virtue in lowliness.

hun (hwun)
see soul.

I Ching (Yi Jing)
The character *I* is the symbol of change. The original meaning of *Ching* is not certain.

jen (ren)
a man.

jen (ren)
as distinguished from *man*, is the principle of being a

man, under which is subsumed benevolence, humanity, and other virtues.

K'an (Kan)
    trigram of *Water*:

repeated, forms hexagram	29:	K'an (Kan)
with Sun above forms hexagram	59:	Huan (Hwan)
with Ch'ien above forms hexagram	6:	Sung (Sung)
with Tui above forms hexagram	47:	K'un (Kwun)
with Li above forms hexagram	64:	Wei Chi (Wei Ji)
with Chen above forms hexagram	40:	Chieh (Jye)
with K'un above forms hexagram	7:	Shih (Shr)
with Ken above forms hexagram	4:	Meng (Meng)

K'ANG HSI (KWANG SYI)
    an emperor of the Ch'ing dynasty (1662-1722) during whose reign the *I* was exhaustively edited. The K'ang Hsi dictionary was an achievement of his reign. The imperial K'ang Hsi edition of the *I* appeared in 1715 and contains quotations from 218 scholars from the 2nd century B.C. to 17th A.D.

Ken (Gen)
    trigram of *Mountain*:

repeated, forms hexagram	52:	Ken (Gen)
with K'an above forms hexagram	39:	Chien (Jyan)
with Sun above forms hexagram	53:	Chien (Jyan)
with Ch'ien above forms hexagram	33:	Tun (Dwun)
with Tui above forms hexagram	31:	Hsien (Syan)
with Li above forms hexagram	56:	Lu (Lyu)
with Chen above forms hexagram	62:	Hsiao Kuo (Syau Gwo)
with K'un above forms hexagram	15:	Ch'ien (Chyan)

kuei-shen (gwei-shen)
    Kuei denotes the animal soul or nature and shen the intellectual soul, the union of which constitutes the living rational man. (J.L.)

K'un (Kwun)
    trigram of *Earth*:

repeated, forms hexagram	2:	K'un (Kwun)

with Ken above forms hexagram   23:   Po (Bwo)
with K'an above forms hexagram   8:   Pi (Bi)
with Sun above forms hexagram   20:   Kuan (Kwan)
with Ch'ien above forms hexagram   12:   P'i (Pi)
with Tui above forms hexagram   45:   Ts'ui (Tswei)
with Li above forms hexagram   35:   Chin (Jin)
with Chen above forms hexagram   16:   Yü (You)

K'UNG YING-TA (KUNG YING-DA)
    one of the *I*'s many interpreters.

LAO-TZU (LAU-DZ)
    exact dates not known; contemporary with Confucius. Founder of Taoism.

Li (Li)
    trigram of *Fire*:
repeated, forms hexagram   30:   Li (Li)
with Chen above forms hexagram   55:   Feng (Feng)
with K'un above forms hexagram   36:   Ming I (Ming Yi)
with Ken above forms hexagram   22:   Pi (Bi)
with K'an above forms hexagram   63:   Chi Chi (Ji Ji)
with Sun above forms hexagram   37:   Chia Jen (Chya Ren)
with Ch'ien above forms hexagram 13:   T'ung Jen
                        (Tung Ren)
with Tui above forms hexagram   49:   Ko (Ge)

li (li)
    a philosophical doctrine ostensibly concerned with etiquette and decorum.
    The meanings symbolized by different ceremonies.
    One of the spherical concepts better borrowed into our language than translated, as are "tao," "wu wei," "t'ai chi" and others of both immediate and abstract meaning.

li (li)
    as a unit of measure, equal to about a third of a mile.

Li Chi (Li Ji)
    Book of Rites, one of the five classics.

LIANG YIN (LYANG YIN)
    scholar, interpreter of the *I Ching*.

limits
    "Exceeding the proper limits" indicates the knowing to
advance but not to retire; to maintain but not to let perish;
to get but not to lose. (J.L.)

the Master
    refers to Confucius.

mean
    is the course of moderation. Due mean is the applica-
tion of moderation *moderately*, as moderation carried too far
ceases to be moderate.

MENCIUS
    372-289 B.C.

ming (ming)
    fate; the destiny to which one is called.

ming (ming)
    see: name.

name
    The ming name is used by one's elders. The tzu desig-
nates a courtesy name, used in formal address or by servants. Both the tzu and the ming names are connected in
some way with the official name.

origin
    of the diagrams, of things; see: T'ai Chi.

pa kua (ba gwa)
    the trigrams; from pa meaning eight, and kua meaning
to divine.

PAO-HSI (BAO-SYI)
    see FU HSI.

penetrating, the
assemblage of excellences; by inference: ultimate triumph of good over evil.

place
To "take one's place" means to be neither too humble nor overly ambitious. By "taking one's place," which means both active seeking and inactive meditation, one achieves harmony with the Tao; one moves with "the course of things" in the "great business of life."

p'o (pwo)
see soul.

powers
the Three Powers—Earth, Man, and Heaven; represented by lines 1, 2, and 3 of the trigrams; in the hexagrams by lines 1 and 2, 3 and 4, and 5 and 6—in that order.

pronunciations: (approximations)
a is broad, as in father
e is pronounced as e
i is ye
u is oo
ei: a
ia: ya
ie: ye
ih: r
hs: sh

When followed by an apostrophe, ch, k, p, and t are pronounced as they sound. But when without an apostrophe, they are pronounced:
ch: j
k: g
p: b
t: d

When using a combination of two or more Chinese words, try to imitate a singsong tone. In Chinese, every syllable is pronounced.

When confronted with the impossible, such as tdz or a similar combination: imitate a bumblebee uttering a staccato syllable.

Careful attention to the Yale system of romanization will be of great help in pronouncing Chinese.

propriety
　　not mere ceremony, as propriety without humility fails. This is illustrated by the tradition of li (etiquette) in Chinese philosophy.

regret
　　indicates anxiety. It is a small fault.

repentance
　　The feeling of repentance stirs up the thought securing that there shall be no blame. "Cause for repentance" indicates sorrow. (J.L.)

righteousness
　　right administration of wealth, correct instructions to the people, and prohibitions against wrongdoing constitute righteousness. (J.L.)

Sage rulers
　　The five "sage rulers" are
　　　　FU HSI
　　　　SHEN NUNG
　　　　HUANG TI
　　　　YAO
　　　　SHUN
"Like the clouds and the rain to the thirsty earth, so is the rule of the sage to expectant humanity."

Shang (Shang) (or Yin) (Yin) dynasty:
　　the second dynasty, usually dated from 1766 to 1122 B.C.

shen (shen)
　　are the good spirits of folklore.
　　Also, shen is used to designate all or part of what lies beyond our knowledge.

341

All shen are identified with the yang principle.
See: kuei-shen.

SHEN NUNG (SHEN NUNG)
legendary sage emperor; succeeded FU HSI.

sheng (sheng)
often appears as an adjective, indicating sagely wisdom, righteousness, an ideal condition where what is within matches what appears without.
Sheng jen (sheng ren): a sage.

Shih Ching (Shr Jing)
Book of Poetry, one of the five classics. In point of age, Legge places this book between the *Shu Ching* and the *I Ching*.

shih fei (shr fei)
the concept of opposites.

SHIH HUANG TI (SHR HWANG DI)
founder of the Ch'in dynasty. He unified China and built the Great Wall. In B.C. 213 he ordered the burning of books which became known as the "fires of Ch'in."

Shih I (Shr Yi)
The Ten Wings.

Shu Ching (Shu Jing)
The Book of History, one of the five classics.
It is Legge's opinion that in this work is contained China's oldest writing.

SHUN (SHWUN)
legendary sage emperor; succeeded YAO; reign ended B.C. 2203.

six arts
as cultivated by the ancient Chinese:
1. archery
2. chariot driving
3. correct behavior

    4.   mathematics
    5.   music
    6.   reading and writing

soul
    The Chinese have a dual concept of soul: a spiritual soul, hun, and an animal soul, p'o.
    "At death the hun wanders away, ascending, and the p'o descends and is changed into a ghostly shade. So did the ancient Chinese grope their way from material things to the concept and representation of what was immaterial." (J.L.)
    See also kuei-shen.

SSU-MA CH'IEN (SZ-MA CHYAN)
    author of the *Shih Chi* (Shr Ji), an historical record of more than 500,000 words.
    It is on the authority of Ssu-ma Ch'ien that Legge attributes to king Wen the expansion of the 8 trigrams to 64 hexagrams.
    Circa B.C. 145-88.

ssu tuan (sz dwan)
    the four essentials to humanity: wisdom, benevolence, ceremonies and righteousness.

Sui (Swei) dynasty:
    A.D. 590-620. In this period, under the duke of Sui, China began the emergence from her Dark Ages.

Sun, (Swun)
    trigram of *Wind* and also of *Wood*:

repeated, forms hexagram	57:	Sun (Swun)
with Ch'ien above forms hexagram	44:	Kou (Gwo)
with Tui above forms hexagram	28:	Ta Kuo (Da Gou)
with Li above forms hexagram	50:	Ting (Ding)
with Chen above forms hexagram	32:	Heng (Heng)
with K'un above forms hexagram	46:	Sheng (Sheng)
with Ken above forms hexagram	18:	Ku (Gu)
with K'an above forms hexagram	48:	Ching (Jing)

Sung (Sung) dynasty:
> A.D. 960-1280. One of China's great ages.
> Gun powder was invented. Scholarship and the arts flourished.

"the superior man"
> The superior man learns and accumulates the results of his learning; puts questions, and discriminates among those results; dwells magnanimously and unambitiously in what he has attained to; and carries it into practice with benevolence. (J.L.)

T'ai Chi (Tai Ji)
> (also referred to as Great Extreme, Grand Terminus, Great Expansion, Supreme Ultimate; and also Ridge Pole from an early interpretation of the Chinese characters which was both literal and symbolic.)
> Chu Hsi gives to it the figure of a circle.
> Wang Pi: Existence must begin in nonexistence, and therefore the Grand Terminus produced the two elementary forms. T'ai Chi is the denomination of what has no denomination. As it cannot be named, the text takes the extreme point of anything that exists as an analogous term for the T'ai Chi.
> Legge: "Chi is used for the extreme term of anything, as the ridge-pole of a house, or the pinnacle of a pagoda."

T'ai Chi Ch'uan (Tai Ji Chwan)
> Chinese ceremonial boxing of great antiquity. Its physical expression is symbolic, and probably was used to foster an oral tradition. It is related to the Supreme Ultimate T'ai Chi.
> It is today being practiced all over the world as both a health-giving form of calisthenics and a means of relieving mental tension.

TAI TUNG (DAI DUNG)
> Chinese philologist.

TAN (DAN)
> see CHOU, duke of.

T'ANG (TANG)
  a legendary hero of the line of Hsia.

T'ang (Tang) dynasty:
  B.C. 620-907. China's golden age.

tao (dao)
  as implicit in the *I Ching*, see "course of things."
  Used in this work as Divine Reason, and also as path or course.

teh (deh)
  literally, moral excellence accompanied by power and strength.
  As tao may be said to transform, teh is the result of such transformation.

thicket of thorns
  (Hexagram 29) suggests a prison, and is illustrative of the Chinese ability to communicate by suggestion.

Three Kingdoms, period of
  A.D. 221-265. Comprised of the states of Wu, Wei, and Shu.
  This period marks the beginning of the Dark Ages, when China was overrun by war lords.

three years
  is often used to denote "a long time." (J.L.)

Ti: Sheng Ti (Sheng Di)
      God; "the Lord and Ruler of Heaven"
      Sheng Ti—analogue for God
      Ti—Supreme God

TI YI (DI-YI)
  a sovereign of the Yin dynasty of whom little is known; Legge gives his reign from B.C. 1191 to 1155. He is mentioned in Hexagrams 11 and 54.

t'ien (tyan)
  means both heaven and sky.

t'ien li (tyan li)
    divine law.

tsa kua (dza gwa)
    the 64 hexagrams—tsa meaning mingled, or mixed; variegated.

Tsin dynasty: (Dzin)
    A.D. 265-590. During this time China sank still lower into her Dark Ages. It was a time of utter chaos.

t'uan
    The summary of the idea of the hexagram as a whole. It appears as the first paragraph of the Text. Ascribed to king Wen; B.C. 1143±.

Tui (Dwei)
    trigram of *Marsh*:

repeated, forms hexagram	58:	Tui (Dwei)
with Li above forms hexagram	38:	K'uei (Kwei)
with Chen above forms hexagram	54:	Kuei Mei (Gwei Mei)
with K'un above forms hexagram	19:	Lin (Lin)
with Ken above forms hexagram	41:	Sun (Swun)
with K'an above forms hexagram	60:	Chieh (Jye)
with Sun above forms hexagram	61:	Chung Fu (Jung Fu)
with Ch'ien above forms hexagram	10:	Lu (Lyu)

two elementary forms
    the yang and yin symbols of the undivided and divided lines produced by the Grand Terminus. From these the hsiang were developed.

tzu (dz)
    see: name.

virtue
    has the meaning of strength as well as goodness. It can also mean either of these two qualities.

WANG PI (WANG BI)
    a noted commentator on the *I Ching*. A.D. 226-249.

WEN, king (WEN)
   founder of the Chou dynasty; author of the t'uan, the paragraphs descriptive of the hexagrams, and comprising the first section of the Text. His contributions date from 1143 or '42 B.C.

Wen Yen Ch'uan (Wen Yan Chwan)
   The Record of Wen Yen. Supplementary to the t'uan and the yao on the first and second hexagrams, and showing how they may be interpreted of man's nature and doings. The Seventh Wing, and fourth appendix in the complete text.

wing
   The literal meaning of this character in Chinese is help. Legge arranged the ten "helps" (Shih I) into seven appendices.
   Throughout the ages, the accretions to the I have been arranged in various ways.

WU (WU)
   an emperor of the line of Shang.

wu chi (wu ji)
   the Infinite, from which t'ai chi emerged.
   The Great Void, being a state of potentiality.
   The symbol of wu chi is the empty circle.

wu ching: (wu jing)
   see: five classics.

wu hsing (wu sying)
   see: five elements.

wu lun (wu lwun)
   the five relationships:
      1.   between the ruler and his subjects
      2.   between father and son
      3.   between husband and wife
      4.   between brothers
      5.   between friends

wu wei (wu wei)
> sometimes called the doctrine of no mind, or mindlessness. It is the practice of personal passivity in order to allow the harmonious workings of tao to fulfill itself.

> It is an example of many Oriental terms which appear transparently simple yet upon reflection reveal bottomless profundity.

Yale system
> is a romanization which both simplifies transliterations from the Chinese and makes the pronunciations easier to sound out.

yang
> a principle, such as positive, male. Also, the sunny slope, what is bright, the sun, day; what is dry, what is warm. The father concept. What is above, what is visible. What is strong and what is hard.
> Acting.
> The obvious.

yang trigrams
> Ch'ien
> Chen
> K'an
> Ken

yao
> duke of Chou's interpretation of the lines of the hexagrams. They are numbered 1 through 6, and follow the t'uan of king Wen (which comprises the first paragraph of the text). Written 30 or 40 years after the t'uan, completed by 1105 B.C.

YAO
> legendary emperor; succeeded Huang Ti.

yin
> a principle, such as negative, female. Also, the shady side of a mountain, what is obscure, the moon, dark; what is moist, what is cool. The mother concept. What is below, what is hidden. What is weak and what is soft.

Thinking.
The obscure.

Yin dynasty
see Shang dynasty.

yin trigrams (yin)
K'un
Sun
Li
Tui

ying (ying)
anything of exceptional beauty. When applied to persons it indicates the virtues as well as outward appearance.

Yinism
thought to be a religion of matriarchal China in the earliest times; a cult of the *mother*, and bringing forth from darkness.

yü wu (yu wu)
being and nonbeing.

Yuan (Ywan) dynasty:
A.D. 1280-1368. During this period, in 1295, Marco Polo visited Kublai Khan and remained for seventeen years. China was then known to the Western world as Cathay.

It is noteworthy, and perhaps indicative of much of China's history, that though the Sung Empire was overwhelmed by the Mongols under Genghis Khan, the museums of the world today house many Sung works of art. Furthermore, the Mongol conquest was dissipated in the next generation by means of a native population explosion which greatly expanded the numbers of the so-called conquered.